D1198357

When one keeps the glad song singing in one's heart
then do the hearts of others sing.

— from the diary of Opal Whiteley

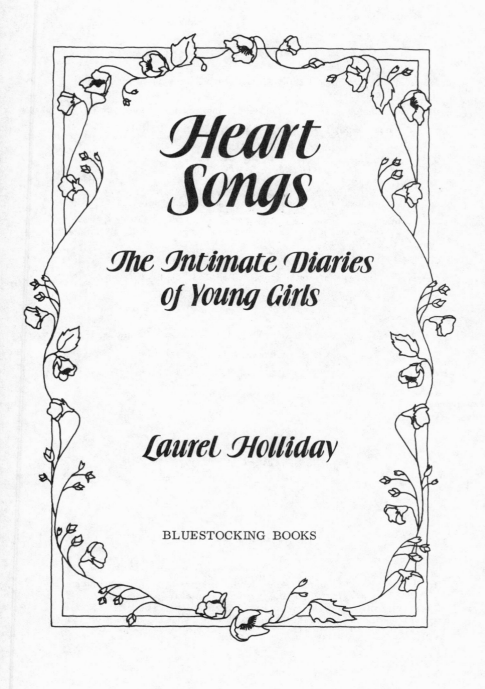

Heart Songs

The Intimate Diaries of Young Girls

Laurel Holliday

BLUESTOCKING BOOKS

Since this page cannot legibly fit all permissions acknowledgments, they are on page six.

The cover design is from a steel engraving by H. Siddons Mowbray.

Book design by Gina Covina and Laurel Holliday.

ISBN 0-931458-00-5
Made in the U.S.A.
1 2 3 4 5 6 7 8 9

Published by BLUESTOCKING BOOKS:
Box 475, Guerneville, California 95446

Distributed by Bookpeople: 2940 Seventh Street, Berkeley, California 94710; and by Women in Distribution: Box 8858, Washington, D.C. 20003.

Library of Congress Cataloging in Publication Data.

Main entry under title:

Heart Songs

  SUMMARY: The diaries of ten girls reveal their adolescent years.
   1. Adolescent girls--Juvenile literature.
2. Diaries--Juvenile literature. (1. Adolescent
girls. 2. Diaries) I. Holliday, Laurel, 1946-
HQ798.H42   301.43'15'0922 (920)   78-17240
ISBN 0-931458-00-5

Bluestocking:
1. a woman with considerable scholarly, literary or intellectual ability or interest. 2. a member of a mid-18th century London literary circle (so called from the informal attire, esp. blue woolen instead of black silk stockings, worn by some women of the group).
                                        — *Random House Dictionary*

Contents

ACKNOWLEDGMENTS:

Marie Bashkirtseff, selections from *Marie Bashkirtseff: The Journal of a Young Artist*, translated by Mary J. Serrano, copyright © 1919 by E. P. Dutton; renewal by Mr. Harold G. Villard. Reprinted by permission of the publishers, E. P. Dutton.

Mathilde von Buddenbroch, selections from *Le Journal de Marguerite*, translated from the German by L. Louis-Filliol, A. Cherbuliez et Comp., Geneva, 1875. Translation from the French especially for this book by Molly Prescott.

Kathie Gray, pseudonym, selections from *Kathie's Diary: leaves from an old, old diary*, edited by Margaret W. Eggleston, copyright 1926 by George H. Doran Co. All possible efforts have been made to locate the current holder of copyright. Anyone who knows of her whereabouts please contact Bluestocking Books so that correction can be made in future editions.

Flora and Benoite Groult, selections from *Diary in Duo*, translated from the French by Humphrey Hare, copyright 1965 by Les Editions Denoel, Paris.

Selma Lagerlof, selections from *The Diary of Selma Lagerlof*, translated by Velma Swanston Howard, copyright 1936 by Doubleday, Doran and Company.

Gretchen Lainer, pseudonym, selections from *A Young Girl's Diary*, first published in 1921, most recent impression copyright 1971 by George Allen and Unwin Ltd., London.

Anais Nin, excerpt from her early diary. Translated from the original French by the author. First published by special permission in the Summer 1959 issue of *Birth*. First printed in book form in *Small Voices*, edited by Josef and Dorothy Berger, New York, 1966. Included in different form in *Linotte: The Early Diary of Anais Nin, 1914-1920*. Copyright 1978 by Rupert Pole as trustee under the last will and testament of Anais Nin. All rights reserved. Reprinted by permission of the author's representative.

Nelly Ptaschkina, selections from *The Diary of Nelly Ptaschkina*, edited by M. Jacques Povolotsky, Jonathon Cape Ltd., London 1923.

Maggie Owen Wadelton, selections from *The Book of Maggie Owen*, copyright 1941 by The Bobbs-Merrill Company, Inc. Reprinted by permission of the publishers.

For Keri and Valerie
and all the little sisters

Introduction

Five years ago, when I was combing the stacks of a university library researching another book, *The Diary of Nelly Ptaschkina* uncannily fell off a shelf directly in front of me, and after glancing through it I couldn't resist reading Nelly cover to cover. So began my love for girls' diaries, which has led me to travel throughout Eastern and Western Europe looking for little-known diaries, and to spend many wonderful hours reading hundreds of girls' diaries from around the world.

I have selected these ten girls for their incredible ability to make me laugh and cry and see parts of myself through their mirror. Highly introspective, articulate girls who range from age eleven to eighteen, they are from Russia, Austria, France, Germany, Switzerland, Sweden, Scotland and the U. S.

Here in their intimate diaries, adolescents themselves describe the experience of sexual awakening, philosophical searching, and cultural transition which sociologists and psychologists have only cut and dried for us. This is the book I was looking for when as a lonely and somewhat lost teenager I tried to find other girls on the library shelves who could help me with what I was going through. Needless to say I never found the accounts I was looking for in my local public library. All of the excerpts included here are from out-of-print or rare books, virtually inaccessible to all but scholars.

Although the girls span five centuries, are from diverse socioeconomic backgrounds and eight different countries, they share concerns which are the same as many young girls' today. The perennial questions of adolescence are explored by the girls in ways which may take us beyond our culture-bound answers. Sex, marriage, the position of women, for example, are considered with a candor and outspokenness which will probably surprise readers today. Mathilde, who lived in the 1500's in Switzerland, had this to say about marriage:

> Marriage, I believe, is an indissoluble bond which obliges the woman to leave everything behind and follow her husband. Really, it's awful.... Marriage is a cage which locks you in, and even if this cage is made of diamonds and gold, it is still a cage.

Benoite, a sophisticated eighteen-year-old living in occupied Paris during the Second World War, echoes Mathilde's sentiments four centuries later:

> It's wholly unjust...for a woman is much better conditioned by her husband than a man is by his wife. For her, the trap of marriage is a precipice. And what lies at the bottom of it? Detergents, ammonia, crackers, floor polish, dust under the beds, the chicken to be put in the pot, care of one's skin and ugly marks to hide, breasts to be held in place and the menopause to undergo, while other girls are growing up in neighboring fields.
> Brrrrr! How does one manage to survive all that?

Witty, outspoken, even brash and caustic at times, still all the girls' hearts remain open to love. They long for it, alternately believing in it and doubting its possibility; most of all, they try to define it. What is "love," this force which drives us beyond our reason, in which we are swept away, knocked off our feet, bedazzled?

Twelve-year-old Maggie is truly puzzled:

> Two days hand running I've seen Edward. I think I have deep love for Edward. I dont know have I or not but there is no one that would not laugh me down did I ask them.

Fifteen-year-old Flora is no more certain, even though she has "kissed a boy on the lips":

> I am madly happy to be a grown-up young girl. My protracted childhood weighed on me and the fact that I am loved is like a consecration of my new state. I cannot, however, make up my mind whether it is Van Buck I love or his love for me. At times, he gets the benefit of my doubt; at others, on the other hand, I am annoyed with him because I don't adore him.

I love these girls, every one of them. They are with me in my thoughts like the houseful of sisters I never had. I hope they'll touch your hearts as they have mine and give encouragement to girls (young and old) to write your heart's songs.

Laurel Holliday

1978

All of the girls' original spelling, punctuation, and grammar have been retained. They are arranged in the order of their ages at the time of writing.

The most famous diary keeper of our times, Anaïs Nin began her writing as a little girl. When her father abandoned her family in Europe, her mother brought her and her brothers to New York City to make a new start. Lonely and very disappointed with city surroundings, Anaïs wrote stories for herself and began a diary which was to be her lifelong companion.

This part of her diary was written when she was eleven; already, adolescent questionings and longings are apparent. She feels that she is different from other children, eccentric, unable to fit in. She knows she is gifted and dreams of one day being a great writer.

Her dream was realized through hard work and a firm belief in herself. After many years of printing her books by hand on a used letter press, she finally convinced the literary world of her talent.

Anaïs Nin gained public acclaim only in the last decade. Her diaries (six volumes in all) have appealed especially to women during a time of rising female consciousness.

She died of cancer in 1977.

1903 - 1977

Anaïs Nin

November 19, 1914

I write here many things I never tell anyone. Today when I opened a book at hazard, I read: "Life is only a sad reality." Is it true? Perhaps! I have never discussed this. Today I want to know, and even though my diary is dumb, I will ask: is it true? Oh, if anyone asked me this on my dark, sad days when I was thinking of father--oh, I would certainly say yes, but that is all. Certainly I have not suffered yet--I am only eleven, and I cannot say; I must wait longer before I can answer this question.

Though my curiosity is not satisfied, I resign myself to talk about other things. When I see a beggar, I want to be rich, merely to help him. I ask myself, how is it possible there should be beggars with so many rich men on earth? Only it is true, many rich men don't give. If I could only give, give! With this idea I gathered all my toys to give to the chapel.

I don't know what is wrong with me. I confess, that

question--is life only a sad reality?--occupies my mind.
Silly idea! No doubt I have many silly notions, many crazy
ones. I know. I admit it. Just the same--I want to know.

January 11

I work hard at school, but that does not prevent me
from doing what I prefer to do. I have written a story,
Poor Little One. I only love either very gay or very sad
things. I hate school, and everything about this new life
in this big city. Mother asked me why. Why? Why?
Because I love silence, and here it is always noisy: because
everything here is somber, shut in, severe, and I love gay
landscapes. I love to see the sky, to admire the beauty
of nature, and here the houses are so tall, so tall one does
not see anything. If you do catch a little corner of the
sky, it is neither blue nor pink or quite white--no, it is a
black sky, heavy, lugubrious, soiled by the pride and vanity
of modern men and women.

I say this because I hate the modern. I would have
loved to live in the first century, in Ancient Rome: I would
have loved to live in the time of great castles and gracious
ladies; I would have loved the time of Charlotte Corday,
when any woman could become a heroine.

I must recognize that I am crazy, but since my diary
is destined to be that of a mad woman, I cannot write reasonable things in it! And they would not be my thoughts.

February 3

How beautiful it is now! It has snowed for days, so
hard that all the streets and houses are white in spite of
the furious work of human beings to take it all away. Even

the sky has taken part in this feast of pure color, and now I love it. But it will last so little, because the snow is being chased away, and the sky will be in mourning again. Everybody pushes it away except the children.

In the classroom, we open the windows when the teacher has her back turned, and we run and fight to catch the snowdrops, and when one of us catches one you see a face blossom into a beautiful smile. I had caught several when the teacher, jealous of our joy, rolled angry eyes, and closed the window. Then all the children went back to their desks, but more determined than ever to come back to the snow some time. I am going to dream about snow and birds, which I love so much.

February 27

I must tell about a singular dream I had last night. I found myself in a grand salon, carpeted in dark gray. I was seated on a small chair which smelled of pine. Then a fine lady dressed in black velvet and wearing a belt of diamonds or something sparkling rushed towards a grand piano on which she played a long, sad melody. It made me sad. Then she stopped, went to a big easel, took a brush, and began to paint. She painted a somber woods, with a pale blue sky in the distance. In one minute she was through. Then she advanced towards a big desk, and taking up a pen and a big book, her big eyes looking at me and then at the sky, she began to write. She wrote pages and pages. I could see they were big and beautiful poems, full of charm, tenderness and sweetness. I could not read them but I feel sure they were beautiful. Then she closed the

book, laid down the pen, and came silently towards me.
And then I heard this word: Choose.

Oh, how much I hesitated! First I remembered the
beautiful melody, then I suddenly turned towards the easel--
it was so beautiful--and with a paintbrush I could describe
the sweet and charming landscapes, all the beauty of nature.
But suddenly I turned towards the big desk, loaded with
books. An invisible force led me towards that corner.
Involuntarily I seized the pen. Then the lady, smiling,
came to me and gave me a big book, saying, "Write. I
will guide you." Without any difficulty I wrote things which
I think were beautiful. Pointing to a corner where men
with venerable beards, as well as queens and pretty ladies
were writing without pause, the lady said, "Your place is
there."

As soon as the lady was gone, I softly put down the
book. I went towards the piano. I wanted to try it. First
my fingers went very well. I liked what I was playing.
But suddenly I had to stop. I did not know any more.
Then, looking at the piano, sadly I thought: I cannot. Then
I tried to paint again. My landscape was already pretty,
but I stopped and saw that big smudges spoiled the whole
thing, and then I said, "Adieu, I don't want this."

Then I took up the pen again, and I began to write
without stopping.

My dream was very long, but it seems so strange, I
want to tell it so as to be able to reread it. Mother is
calling me. I wish I could dream that way again.

May 12

I would like that nobody should ever know me. I would

like to live isolated and alone. I envy the lives of those souls who can feel such peace, such sweetness in solitude. In one of my stories I uncover the sweetness of this solitude which everybody fears. Why? Because they are sick, and blind.

There is one thing which troubles me. I feel different from everybody. I notice no child in my class of my age thinks as I do. They are all alike, they are in accord. I know their thoughts, their ambitions. And I make comparisons. I am altogether different. Instead of being like brothers to me, they are strangers. My desires, my dreams, my ambition, my opinions, are different. Why am I not like everybody?

Glancing over this notebook, I said to myself, "Yes, these are my thoughts, but they are contrary. Am I what is called an eccentric, an "original" as the French say? Must I be looked upon by the world as a curiosity? Certainly I do not seek to contradict what people think, and still, when I reread these pages, I think my feelings are contrary to what is called happiness. When I reread these pages I like to be able to say, "This is a special story. Does it matter if no one understands? Am I writing for the world? No. My language is unknown. What a joy it will be if I am overlooked! Then my treasures will belong to me alone. When I die I will burn these pages and my thoughts scribbled here will live only in eternity with the one who expressed them!"

But of course, if someone should understand, if someone should hear this contradictory language, these novel impressions, I would be very happy indeed.

Maggie Owen Wadelton

Maggie was born in Ireland at the turn of the century to a wealthy family, but she was never to really know her parents since they both died when she was a small child. She grew up in castles and mansions with relatives and friends who were delighted with the company of such a cheerful, loving girl.

She was a natural comedian who was all the funnier for being completely unaware of her gift. The more seriously she takes the small events which come to her, the more hilarious is her description of them. Although she showed her book only to those she loved, she seems to have written with her readers in mind . . . . never boring, always clearly explaining everything, and developing her characters with vivid detail like a novelist.

When Maggie grew up she did, in fact, become a writer. A description of Maggie grown-up can be found in a book written by her twelve-year-old son, Thomas, tellingly entitled My Mother is a Violent Woman.

1897 - 1972

Maggie Owen Wadelton

January 24, 1908

This is me birthday and I consider me New Year begins this day instead of January first. Anyways I was given this book for a present and a gold soverign along with it, a prayer book also that I have too many of. I start this book this day and shall put down me best thoughts and all important things that happen to me--if any do--and what I learn at me lessons. I call it a Year Book instead of a Diary because Diary sounds like a running off of the bowels and is vulgar. Me name is Marget Owen, a fine name would anyone call it me. Always they call me Maggie-Ane or Peg, I dont know why Owen is called Ane. I think theres many a thing I'll have to find out.

I am a virgin twelve years of age. Spinster and demoselle and maiden mean the same thing, but not quite. I call meself a virgin and it sounds higher minded and more

21

spiritual. I resolve to be a noble woman but tis hard to
be noble in a house along with people not noble. They
dont want to be noble and hinder me spiritual efforts with
teasing. All the well known people you read of have trouble with their families. Look at Joan of Arc and Queen
Elizabeth and St. Terese. Their families dident understand them when they started to be noble so they went away
from their families. No one understands me either. Some
day I will leave Castel Rea and go out in the world and
me name will ring down the corridors of time no doubt.

These are me resolves for 1908,

I shall lead a noble life always, am I let.

I shall learn something new each day.

I shall not wrestle with the food caught in me teeth,
are there others about that would see me.

I shall be gentle in me mein (this is a new word and
means how you look when other people look at you).

I will be more lady like and not get into fights can I
help it.

I will be diligent in me tasks and not fall asleep when
I say me prayers.

There was a fine party last night and Bess had me sit
on the stairs late to watch the ladies and gentlemen come
in kerreges.

I wakened in the night and heard singing. One lady
wore a fine pink silk gowen, she comes here often. Ann
says she has no purpose in life and is a silly young woman.
Wherever she is the gentlemen all gather about her. She
takes her fences the like of a feather in the wind when
she hunts. Last night I saw her kissed below the stairs

which is a sin.

Sister Mary-Bernard says the sins of the world creep on us when we least expect them so I think that is the reason I thought of the lady with the pink silk gowen all the day long. Her name is Norah. When the gentlemen kissed her she looked bothered. When I love twill be different. Twill be a noble love. Save I go into a convent, then I must put all thought of the flesh behind me. It is a noble life devoted to good works and I think I'd look fine in the costume they wear. I have large eyes in the face, grey ones, and I can make a rapt expression easily enough, though twould be hard on me to go around looking rapt all of the time. Me ears stick out but the wimple would cover them no doubt. I pinned a white towel around me head for the wimple and the bottom of a black skirt for the veil. It looked fine from the front but stuck out in the back.

Tonight is a beautiful night and moonlighted. I looked out the window for long in meditation. Ann sent me here in punishment for losing me temper and getting me eye blacked in a fight. Tis hard to be a noble character when they pick on me. Ann says I'm too big a girl to fight but I doubt if I'd got off with only one black eye had I been smaller.

Ann says tis shamed she is because Vincents mother sent over a note saying Vincent was on the broad of his back with the hurt I put on him and maybe he'll have the doctor to him. Twas Vincent gave me the eye. He sneaked up behind me with a cold pigs tail and dropped it down me back and away with him, and I after him. I caught him

up and licked the porrige out of him. I got the eye and
me drawers were torn off me almost on a hedge. I lar-
ruped him well. He got a bloodied nose and I am glad of
it. Nothing can stop me from being glad of it am I kept
here forever.

Were I the mother of a lad with twelve and three quarter years over his head and he licked bad by a girl with
but twelve years and four days to her name, I'd keep it
like a secret of the dead and not go and annoy the neighbors
with notes written about it and trouble made for the innocent. A black imp of hell is Vincent and it not a lie that
I write.

Me eye is black. Tis glad I am that I'm serious about
me Year Book, tis a great comfort to me. I've started
journals oft before but they never lasted as long as this.
Tis older and more responsible I am. Me life is hard to
bear with every one picking fun at me eye. Did I not have
a strong character I'd cry no doubt. I want with all me
soul to be a noble and great character, but there will be
no skylarking around and pigs tails down me back without
me having something to say.

I read Victor Hugos book Les Misriables and I not
supposed to read it. An odd book. It says Fanchon gave
herself as to a husband. She had a child. I wonder how
you can give yourself to anyone. If I ask about it the book
will be taken and I'll be punished for reading pugutorious
writing.

After tea I learned a new word. The word I learned
was Lycanthrope--one who has been changed to a wolf or
has the power to so change himself. I'll wager a penny

Vincent wishes he could be a Lycanthrope does the big omethaune know there is such a thing.

I wish I was fourteen. I think tis going to school I'll be when I'm fourteen. I will be a growen woman. My mother was married at fourteen, I was born when she was but fifteen. She's dead. My father is dead too, God rest them.

I'd like to marry a tall handsome man that had jet black hair and a kindly nature. He should have a moustache no doubt and they stylish, though I dont like the taste much. Tims tastes always like whiskey. I dont think money special but I'd like him to be a landed gentleman and have a lake with white swans and a boat that I could sit in under a lace parasole and drag me hands in the water. Some lillies in it too. There is a beautiful picture the like of that in the morning room.

I'd like to have nine children. Girls with fine blond curls and boys with dark black hair the like of their father. Not many boys, I dont like boys much.

There is a new boy in the town visiting his uncle. He is an English boy. His name is Edward. He wears golf breeches with tassels to them at the knees, and fancy stockings. He has skinny legs. He was long sick, it well may be tis the sickness made him skinny. His uncle brought him to call and Ann says he has beautiful manners. I am poor mannered, I slopped me tea on me good wool frock and was scolded afterwards. Ann says tis no wonder the British think us barberryians.

I think it well may be this book will fall to the hands
of me grandchildren or me great-grandchildren and they'll
wonder what I was like. I will set down what I am like
for them. I have red hair with curls to it and wish Ann
would let me thrust it up. Twelve years is almost a woman
growen, Standing with reluctant feet where the brook and
river meet (by Alfred Lord Tenneyson I think.) It means
the time when a girl begins to be a woman and not a girl
any more. I have great grey eyes and a nose that turns
up but looks all right. Ann says I have a good skin, did
I take care of it and not run wild and get burned the like
of a red Indian. Me ears are not excellent but you cant
see them with all the hair I have. No one will ever see
them, not even when I'm married to me husband, if I get
one. Bess says husbands are getting scarcer every day.
I am four feet in heighth and weigh six stone. I am not
beautiful now as when a child, me photografs show me very
beautiful then though simpering. I am good at me lessons
when I put me mind to them. I am a sensitive child and
no wonder with the affliction I had on me.

Vincent is out of his bed. I think I did not kill him
entirely. He came over the like as if nothing happened and
said Edward was simple and I said he wasent and we were
on the edge of another fight.

Edward thinks it would be nice to be married to me
but says I'd have to go to live in India as he's to be an
army officer the like of his father. I am an adventurous
child and would like to go off all of the time. I would like
to come back to visit with a long gowen I'd have to hold up
when I got out of the kerrege, and with a fine silk petti-

coat that would rustle, and a veil. I'd like to have four of me children along with me, girls with big hats and streamers down their backs.

I asked Edward would he like to have some children with me and he acted odd and did not answer me.

This was a fine bright day. Crofty brought the horses and I rode forth with Crofty and Ann. A grand ride could I be by meself. Ann catches me up about me riding manners. She says God knows why I dont ride better as I come from horse people that rode when they were diapered. Ann called Crofty up to ride on one side of me and she on the other and all of the time they spoke of me ill riding and told me to do this and do that till twas muddled I was.

I suppose tis fitten I should have manners for the hunt not to disgrace a riding family but God knows tis a lot of bother. I like to go to the paddock by meself and take along sugar, can I get it, or a handfull of oats and the first horse that comes for it is the horse I take. I like to have the lads saddle the horse, not Crofty who always talks too much, and then up and away with me. I like to thrust up me skirt till I can feel the wind blow on me legs and let me hands do what they feel like doing. I like a fine gallop on a stretch with the wind tossing me hair and I like to take a hedge clean and not bother about how I do it so long as I'm well over it.

Edward took me for a long walk by the water before our tea and we talked of serious matters. Edward would like to marry me but he is a Prodestand and I a Catholic and we cant see how it can be come over. Neither of us will budge an inch.

Two days hand running I've seen Edward. I think I
have deep love for Edward. I dont know have I or not but
there is no one that would not laugh me down did I ask them.

Sister Mary-Bernard was cross with me. She said I
did badly with me tasks and that me mind was not on them.
I'm fearfull that nobleness has run out of me and I dont
know why. I'll make better efford and see what will happen. I have done no noble act or thought no noble thought
or learned no new word in many a day. My heart is full
of Edward. I'm fearfull I love him. I asked Sister Mary-
Bernard what would happen to the soul of one that would
marry a Prodestand and she closed her eyes like it hurt
her. She said to get on with me tasks. I expect they
would be dammed forever in hell. It well may be I could
have some fun before I was dammed. No doubt tis better
not to think of the like.

We had guests to tea. Bess put me into the brown
calico that I dont like much, but tis the first spring dress
I've been let to wear and she let me have me pinny with
real lace and a great sash behind. I looked fine. I thought
Edward had come to tea.

I went down and there was Vincent and his aunt. I
was angered and annoyed and hated every bone in his body.
Glad enough to see his aunt but that lad! I'd poison him
could I and not go to hell for it. Twould be hard to suffer
everlasting fire just for getting shut of the likes of him.
I had to be polite or I knew Ann would take it out on me

later.

I hoped Vincent would drip his tea on his best clothing. He wanted that I should sit on the stool by the fire. I would not. I could not but think of me love for Edward and I'd not have the stool made unholy with Vincents behind.

I think I'll pray for Edwards conversion so tis I can marry him. I'll tell him first, tis sneaking to pray behind ones back. I love Edward with all me heart. I want to be a noble woman for him and have him for me nine childrens father. I think nine a fine number. Had I a sister or brother I'd be a happy one. I have no one. Bess thinks tis what makes me an odd child, being lone as I am.

When I waked this day I knew there was something amiss with the world. I examined me conscience but there wasent a spot on it. Mostly when I wake troubled tis somewhat done the day before bothers me... Bess laid out me clothes and put out the dark black frock that I have for Good Friday and me heart stood still within me. I could stand it no longer and cried out what was it. Bess said I'd know soon enough. I ate me porrige and afterward was taken to Ann and may the good Lord have mercy on us all. Tim was dead and cold with a fall he took as he rode home last night in the dark along with Ann from Glebe House. Everyone took on and cried save Ann and she sat cold as the corps itself. I think she's dead inside of her. Ann took me that I'd see Tim lying decent in his own bed with his hands crossed and a crucifix in them. It was a dred thing and I puked over me frock and the floor, and the world went dark. I waked in me bed with Ann and the

doctor and Bess near to me. I started to cry and lament
all over again till Ann lay down by me and soothed me.
She said Tim was with his God and I was not to care so
hard. She said Tim was an aged man and it was time the
both of them thought of going to their reward. I went off
to sleep and I waked to find the day far on toward tea time
and the doctor with me again. He said I must not stay in
the house of death with people coming and going to annoy
me. I'm to be off to where I choose for a visit.

Sister Mary-Rose and Mary-Bernard came and said
would I like to go to them. I would not. I want to go to
Edwards house but I'll say naught for fear there would be
shame put on me. Bess said would I go to her mothers
and have the children to play with. I would not. There's
too many to a bed and they rough children. I'll go nowhere
but to Edwards or I'll bide here and they'll not budge me.

Me book was left behind and I brought here but I havent
needed the book anyway, I'm down with a sickness on me.
I am at Edwards house and Bess is along with me. Twas
not fitting I should be here alone with two gentlemen and
they not married. I dont know how twas I got here but I'll
have it out of Bess soon no doubt.

This is the most elegant room ever I saw and I'd like
to stay here forever. Twill be Edwards some day when the
Major is done with it, so it well may be it will be mine
also, if I live long enough. I have the grandest bed in the
world with pink silk curtains to it. There is a grand soft
rug on the floor with blooms like cabbages, that big they
are, blooms I never saw the like of. It well may be they
are English blooms.

Today was a great day. I was out of me bed for a-
while. Bess had me washed and in a clean robe and Edwards uncle brought a grand fluff of feathers and silk, the
like I never saw, and put it on a small sofa. I was wrapped
in it and lay there the like of a Queen. Me legs are skinny as Edwards. Bess says I'm no heavier than a dressed
goose at Christmas time.

Edwards uncle is named Lord Leak-Standing, but it is
not said that way, it is said Leastening. I dont know is he
a Christian, because he is Prodestand. Does Uncle Mal-
colm not marry and beget, Edward will be his heir. Wealth
makes no matter. I'd love Edward were he a tinker, but
I like this room.

I showed me journal to Edward this day. Edward
thought it remarkable a young girl had written it. I'm glad
he said girl and not child. He's but three years older,
four maybe. He has a birthday soon. He says he'll help
me with me journal. He will not. I love him dearly but
tis me own book and were anyone to help it wouldent be
mine.

Today I asked about Ann and there was no hurt in me
heart when I thought of Tim and him gone to his God, so
tis well I am no doubt. Sore news was given me. Ann
lies in her bed and no bit or sup has passed her lips since
they laid Tim in the graveyard. May the Lord have mercy
on him. Nothing but the physic they force on Ann does she
swallow. I dont know what is to become of me barring tis
the convent I'll be sent to and I dont fancy that. Do they
try it I'll scream again and that'll fix it no doubt. God

forgive me! I think theres not an ounce of nobleness left within me.

This day I was to visit Ann. The visit was put off, I dont know why. Edward rushed in at tea time with the smell of horses on him. Me heart lept. He gave me a kiss. Twas the first time a boy kissed me and if thats all theres to it, a great todo is made about nothing. Edward says he can marry me in six years. He'll be an officer with enough money to look after a family properly, he comes into property of his mothers when he's of age. He says six years is no time at all. I expect in the face of eternity tis not, but it seems long to me. I expect in six years I'll have me speech genteel. Tis a happy woman I am. I think tis betrothed I am.

The day was long. I expect tis the way I'll feel when Edwards me husband and he goes off to his sports and what not without me. Bess says tis a womans place to keep the house for the gentleman and see to his comfort. That is what marriage is for. I'm thinking theres more than that to it or the ladies would not be so forward about it. I'll find out some day meself no doubt. I'll not stay home all of the time I'll tell you.

Tis dark night and no sign of Edward or Uncle. They were to be home this day barring accident. I hope tis not drowned they are. If twas so Edward was drowned would I be a widow? Widows wear black for the rest of their days in respect to their holy dead. I wouldent like that. I like gay colours. Even if I wore no black gowen me heart

would be black with sorrow were I widowed. I wouldent
like to be widowed. Twould be hard on me and me not
married and all.

No word of Ann and no word of Edward. Sure nobody
gives a dam what becomes of me. I used to swear like
the tinkers before I gave it up and became noble but I'll
begin swearing again. Theres no one to care am I noble
or not.

I waked with a joyfull feeling and threw open the case-
ment. I went down to me breakfast and there were Edward
and Uncle eating their meal as if they'd never left the house.
Edward said Lazybones. I was so glad within me I thought
I was going to puke sure but held it in and said good morning properly. God is good.

Never was there such a day. I do love Edward.
Theres no one I have fun or enjoyment with the like of him.
I do hope he'll marry me that we can go on having enjoyment
all of our lives. Tis near to killing me that he's to go off
to school. It well may be he'll forget me entirely, what
with his books and all to fill his head. Twould kill me and
break me heart did he so. He says I should pay such
thoughts no heed at all, that never will he do such a thing.

Twelve-year-old Kathie Gray began her journal one hundred years ago in Ohio. She wrote long detailed entries, probably because she was so often lonely, all her brothers and sisters having died when she was a little girl, and her father living a long way off. Her best friend, Jessie, became a sister to her, but when Jessie's family moved Kathie had to tell all her adventures to "Madam Looking Glass," as she whimsically dubbed her diary.

Kathie Gray is a pseudonym; when she was an elderly woman "Kathie" selected these passages from her diary and published them for young girls. Details of her life after the diary are unknown.

Despite her obvious problems with spelling, she was a good and faithful diarist who wrote voluminously until her wedding day in 1886, when she apparently needed "Madam" no longer.

Kathie Gray

January 19, 1876

Today I am twelve years old and I have commenced my Journal. Cousin Allie is going to help me spell hard words today to start with for she is at home with a sore throat. I love to write but I can't spell well at all and I despise arithmetic. My other lessons are just fine.

Allie says to start my Journal I should tell who I am and all. My name is Katharine Gray and most every one calls me Kate or Kathie and Cousin Bert, who is a big tease, calls me Katy-did because he says I get into so many scrapes. I surely don't mean to but it just seems as if the more I try to be good sometimes, the more things happen. I live in the country because its much healthier than in the city where I was born. Mama and I are all there are of us for my Little Brothers and Baby Sister all died in the city and my Papa isn't with us. I

can't talk much about that even in my Journal which Allie
says is for our very special thoughts. I don't understand
it well at all and it is one thing that I can't ask Mama,
Aunt Mary says, for it makes her very sad. I know this
any way--a boarding school is a very poor place to bring
up babies in and when all her others had died and Uncle
Doctor said to take me straight to the country or I wouldn't
live either why Mama just did it. She *had* to keep *one*.
I know how that is with kittens and ones own little four
year old girl is much more important yet. Mama *had* to
do it.

January 21

I want to *begin* to tell you what a darling *Jessie* is.
We have been fast friends since we were 3 and 4 years
old. I am a year the oldest. Her mother is a "widdow
indead" as the Bible says, and Jessie can talk about her
Papa to any one. He was a discipel minester and her
Mama was a vary good teacher and is so nice. She and
Mama are so conjenial. O how hard to have them moove
away. We write every two weaks--that is I write then
Jessie answers 2 weeks after and then I wate 2 weaks and
write again. Her Grandpa and Grandma live near Aunt
Marys and we will always be together in vacashuns; that
is my only hope.

February 14

Oh I got a precious letter from Jessie and a valentine
in it she made herself. It is very pretty but the letter
was the best--it sounded just like her sweat self. I almost jumped out of my skin when I got it. She called me

her Dear Precious friend and Pet and Dear Darling Katie
And Precious and at the end she said Of coarse I like my
new playmate Mamie but dont ever think I can ever find
in the biggest citty any one that can ever fill your place
in my hart. Isnt that lovely Journal? I am so happy.

February 27

 I have been reading such a pretty fary story about a
magic stone and how if one sat down on it and wished 5
wishes for themselves they would turn to stone and have
to stay there till some one wished them off. If one wished
for some one else they would break the magic spell. The
right way was to do it half and half--only wishing part for
them selves, then both would get what they wanted. Then
I thought if only that big stone in the brook by the stone
bridge was a magic one just what I would do. First I
would wish that Mama might live to be 109 years old. I
prey for that every night any way. Second that I might
have a fairy godmother. Third that I might have it arranged so that I could fly right into Jessie's house and be
inviseble to every one but Jessie. 4--That Jessie could
have it fixed up the same way and no one to see her but
me. 5--That Mama might have all her wishes granted,
every single one. Then I would ask my Fairy Godmother
to give me a magic gobblet and she would tell me in any
trubble to take the gobblet and call on her and she would
come to help me. She would hand it right out to me and
a magic glass to. Any time I wanted to see what Jessie
was doing all I would have to do would be to look in the
magic glass. If I wanted to see what people were doing
in Asia or Africa all I would have to do would be to say

Asia--Africa--and I would see all the strange things--what
people in those countrys were doing just then.   Then my
lovely fairy god-mother would give me the *cunningest* little boy fairy so when I wanted to go to visit Jessie I
would have to but touch him with my wand she left me.
Then he would grow bigger and bigger til he was lotts
larger than I.   Then he would rap me in his wings and in
a minute we would be at Jessie's house.   Then I would
have a beautiful talk with Jessie and would touch my gobblet to wish Jessie might have all the fairy fixing I had--
and a Godmother to.   Then the fairy godmother would say
Goodby and I would Thank her and she would leave me
sitting on the stone.   Then I would gather up all my tre-
sures and touch my boy fairy again and he would rap me
in his wings and we would glide quietly home.   Then I
would say Good night dear little fairy and he would smile
and say Good night little earth child touch your gobblet
when you want me and I will come so fast.   Then I would
see him fly away to the hart of some lovly rose where he
would sink to rest.   Then the fairy bells would tole Goodnight.   The birds would tril their parting lay as they flew
to their sheltered nests amid the drooping leaves.   Then
with a happy hart I to would sink to rest.   This is just
what I wish wish, wish--for then I could get to see Jessie.
I miss her so I just hardly can stand it.

April 4
    O dear Journal I am so excited I cant sit still.   But
I must tell you first that Mama and I went to the Sunday
School Convenshun in Wilton at the new church.   They have
the grandest organ its just lovely and I enjoyed the musik

but the BEST thing happened in the evening. As Mama and
I got off the cars and came round to the front of the depo
there was Jessies grandpa with his carriage and Oh Oh
there was Jessie dearie just getting in. Yes my precious
Jessie come for 1 week of vacashun. Oh didnt we hug and
kiss. She is coming down first thing tomorrow morning.
Oh I am so happy--Happiness will not express my joyful
feelings.

Apr 5.   Eve about 8 o'clock.

Jessie came today at eleven. I had my lessons all
done. I saw her come in the gait and rushed out and we
were *clasped* in each others arms (Jems of Brittish Poetry).

For a few minutes we talked as fast as we could and
both together then we grew more subdooed and got in the
big rocking chair together and talked over everything that
had happened since we parted. Then I showed Jessie what
kittens are left and Jerusalem the Golden and the baby calf.
Next we got all my dolls down from the cupboard, for Jessie is a year younger than I and hasnt put hers away yet
for her grandchildren. Then it was dinner time and being
so happy made us hungry and we ett (no--ate) and ate.
Annie had made ginger cookies and there was new mapel
sirrup too. Mama and Aunt Mary were very glad to see
Jessie. Allie was away--to bad. Then we went for a walk
to the old beach tree and the grape vine swing and Jessie
sang every song she had learned in school for me. Then
I asked Jessie to name the little brook and the pond for it
will comfert me when she is gone again. She named the
brook Arborite River (A grand name for so little a thing)
and the pond Grape Vine Lake. Next we visited Nettie and

plaid on the piano and jumped on the hay and had lots of fun. We went over to the school house and tried to get in a window but could not. Jessie thought she would like to go in and sit in the seat where she used to.

Jessies Mama said she could stay all night with me. We have both been writing in our Journals. Jessie sits just opisit me. She is just as pritty and sweat as ever. She has stoped writing now and has begun to untie her shoes so Goodnight.

Apr 6.

I will commence where I left off. Though it was not very late--nine O'clock--we felt we could not bare to waiste the time sleaping. Jessies vacashun would so soon be gone. So we just took off our heavy shoes and put on our slippers, put out the lamp and just had the lovely firelight most as bright as day. We set our music box going and lay down close to the fire for a blisful rest. Jessie loves the music box Papa brought me from Switszerland. It plays so sweatly four tunes--the battle cry of freedom, Wer War Galop, haste to the wedding and another I cant pronounce-- its forign. Its such *pritty* music. Mama came in then and said we would get to tiard and really must go to bed. We got on our nighties and said Our Father in consert and then each said our own little prayer out loud. Jessie said a *very* sweat prayer and we talked about praying. She said while we were knealing down it just seamed as if God had his arm around us and I thought so to. Then Mama came and tucked us up in bed and Kissed us Goodnight. Dear Mama she loves to have us so happy. Then we named the bed posts each the name of any boy we liked. The one we

looked at first in the morning would be our fate. The big
girls do this. Of coarse its silly but just for fun. Jessie said she didnt know but one nice boy and that was her
cousin Johnnie he didnt plage one all the time. So she
named *all* her posts for him. We both feel so sorry I
haven't any brother and she hasnt either. If we had one
which ever had him would see he married the other one
for we SO want to be related. That would make us *in laws*
any way. Then Mama wrapped and said "Go to sleap Girl-
ies" so we did.

April 10

Jessies visit was lovelier every day and I could not
stop to write about it we were so buisy. She has gone and
left me all sad and lonely. I love her so it seams as
though I could hardly live without her and I shall sing Joy
Joy Joy when she comes again.

April 11

I did lessons and went to Arborite River and Grape-
vine Lake and just felt so lonesome. I just cried my pillow sopping wet last night. Jessie left this little poem for
me.

> *Changes must come*
> *Friends must part*
> *But distance cannot*
> *Change the hart.*

Tuesday, Apr. 18

Its perfectly lovely out of doors now. Nettie and I
went for the wild flowers. We got pink white blue and lav-

ender hipaticas and a few adder tongs and Spring Beuties.
We also found a rabits nest with three cuning baby rabits
in it. We didnt tell Ed or *any* boy.

April 25

O Journal I made such a mistake today. I feal so bad
about it. I beged Mama to go wild flowering with Nettie
and me just as Jessies mother goes tramping with her and
when she said "I cant walk so far Kathie" I fretted a little.
When I came out Aunt Mary looked very solem and told
me I had made my dearie Mama feel sad. Then she said
ever since little baby brother Freddie--who died long ago--
was a *tiny* baby Mama has had a laim side and it often
aches very hard yet she is so chearful. I went right back
where Mama was sowing on my new dress and put my
arms tight about her neck and said the chorus of one of
Allies lovely songs--This is it. "But my Darling you will
be--will be--always young and fare to me." Mama huged
me hard and we cried a little and then we were all happy
again.

April 27.

Oh dear Journal I am so unhappy today. I have a
cold in my head and I cant hear well at all. Everybody's
voice sounds so far away and quear and I dont make out
what they say half the time. I shant go near Nettie and
hope she wont come down for I dont want any of the girls
to know. It just frightens me that I dont hear our big
clock that tick tocks so loud or the robbins either and I
just see Halicausus mew I dont hear him at all. Oh what
shall I do if I stay deaf always?

April 28

Just as I wrote that yesterday Mama came in and saw a tear splash on the page. Oh she was so lovely. She cudled me just as when I was a little girl, said she was sure the deafness would go away soon as my cold did and the only thing now was to be brave and patient and fill up the time while we waited. She said now was the very day to write because one could always think best when it was quiet. I dont just see it for this quiet *scarres* me. I told her so and then how I cried. She said, "Darling we will tell the Heavenly Father all about it." She did and I felt lots better and then we learned a new verse about how they that wait upon the Lord shall renew their strength (Strength of hearing that means too) and about mounting up with wings as eagles, when one is well again (I know just how that means. Its fealing so well and so happy that one can hardly keep from flying off.) Oh thats a very helpful verse. Then I went for violets and we took them and some jelly and went to see Sherrys grandma who is blind-- but she is so plesent and chearful. Deafness isnt *quite* so hard as blindness any way.

April 29.

I haven't one single thing to write about today and yet some way its just what I want to do. I told Mama this and she said write about something I want to remember always that happened before I began to keep a Journal and if I took panes she would count it as a composition. Guess I will.

Aunt Mary has a lovely lusterware tea set which used to be my Grandmas, such cunning shaped sugger bowl and

tea pot and pitchers. Always once in a long while when
we had been very good Allie and I used to have a play tea-
party with these dishes. We both just love pritty things
and it was such fun. Then it was washed *so* carefully and
put back upon the two top shelves of the best dish cubbord.
When I was about seven my favorite Bible Story was about
Joseph and his coat of many collers and his getting to be
a ruler and so nobely saving his brothers who had been so
mean to him when there was an auful famine in the country
where they lived. How they were going to starve to death
and he gave them corn to make bread. Well I always loved
bread and butter espeshally the way Mama fixed it for me
some-times, with scraped mapel sugger on it and sprinkles
of cream on top of that.

Um-m-m that makes me hungry just writing it down
even right after breakfast. I always hated crusts but I was
supposed to eat them of course. Then I had a bright idea.
I thought I would *save every crust* of my between meals
lunches--save them all safely in the Grandma tea set which
nobody looks at only once in a long while and then when
we had a famine in our country--as we might have most
any time--I would climb up in the cubbard and bring out
these crusts and say See my starving family what I have
saved for you. Then they would fall on my neck as they
did on Josephs in the Bible and say O Kathie wasnt that
wonderful of you and other starving folks would wish *their*
little girl had saved her bread crusts for the days of famine. Well it was a lovely plan but it didnt work for when
Aunt Mary was hurrying to get down the dishes because
the new m. e. minister was coming to tea she found the
sugger bowl, tea pot and every covered dish crammed full

of moulded crusts--aufully moulded and smelly. She felt cross and gave me a shakeing. Even now when I am twelve I think that was too bad for I really tried to do a nobel deed (as well as get rid of eating crusts until I had to) and I neerly broke my neck more than once climbing up in a hurry to hide them before any boddy came in.

April 30.

Mama liked my true story but my! what a list of words she got out of it for my spelling lesson today.

May 1.

Oh Journal dear I can *hear the clock tick,* not real loud yet but some--and I heard a robin sing "Cheer up! Cheer up!". Oh I am "mounting up with wings as an eagal" and I am going up to Netties and stay 1 hour.

May 15

Oh Journal Mr Patton has chopped down our wonderful big old beech tree! Oh I could cry a week if that would put that lovley tree back. I was rageing around (for we children loved it so) and Aunt Mary said, "Well Kathie the tree was on Mr Pattons land and it was his" and I said "It was God's first and he tended it for years and years to make it so grand and beautiful and it was WICKED to chop it down!" When we get calmer we mean to speak to Mr Patton about it. They do say part of it is to be sawed into chunks to burn in the m. e. heater to warm the church. If they burn our darling beech tree for that I just wont go to church this winter!! Oh I cant! I cant! Mama wouldnt make me. A lot of us had a sort of funerel in the medow over the poor beautiful tree. Eddie found a birds nest by it with the smashed bits of blue eggs. Oh dear! The robins had just started their house keeping in the big, safe branches. I took Jems of Brittish Verse over there and read out loud, Woodman Spare That Tree, then we all cried (or nearly all most did) and took little chips of our dear old friend home with us to keep.

June 12

Oh dear! Jessie and her Mama have to make another visit first before they come to Menton and its harder than ever to stand it without my darling sister-friend. I thought she would get here next week. Maybe it will make me feal better to write about her. We were together always and loved each other with more than a love. She was my very Idel and I was compleatly *crushed* most a year ago when she mooved away. I was dispondent, suffering agony. Many times last winter I would wake up after dreaming we were together and cry my pillow *Sopping Wet* and get up in the morning with a dull Led pain lying on my hart. I dont think I have yet recovered all my Beuance of Spirit. How I want a picture of my precious Jessie! I will try to write one. She has dark brown wavy hair--long--and so pretty and dark blue eyes and rosy lipps and perfeckly formed fetures. Her nose tilts up *just* the *least* bit. I love it just that way! She is loving ardant conjeanial will stand up for a friend through thick and thin, bright and sparkling brave and dareing great lover of nature and all beautiful things lover of reading lover of poetry generous to a fault and one of those tender romantic ardant natures that we so seldome find.

July 22

Jessie darling has been here a weak and we have had a glorious *scrumpshus* time.

Jessie and I have had the nicest time adopting a child. She and I so admire a big famely and we each mean to have eight or a dozen children when we grow up. We know just how to bring them up but its hard to wait--and that's one thing our mothers wont do for us--they wont adopt a baby. Our child we adopted is named Frances Fidealia Bell Coates. We didn't name her and we call her Frankie for short. She is five years old and so *little*. She has a long narrow little face, the weaest red mouth and a tiny nose and small shy brown eyes and a little yellow pig tale. I wish we dared cut that off--it would be more becoming-- but she is only ours till school is over and when she comes to visit us and her mother might like to keep her hair on.

July 30

Dear Journal--I have to neglect you with school and Jessie and our sewing for Frankie and all. Our poor little child had such shabbie clothes and our Mamas got interested and fixed some of our things over for her and we worked on them too which was lotts more fun than making dolls dresses or hemming towels. Saturday we borrowed Frankie for all day. She *loves* belonging to us and we are just as loveing to her and try out our ideas of govurnment we shall have with our 8 and 12. (I am going to have the 12.) First our Mamas helped us to fix up some toys that we could spare--glewing on parts and so fourth. Just think Journal that child never had a doll just an old shawl tied up for a play baby--and then we borrowed her. Her mother let her go home from school with us to Aunt Marys and Jessie stayed over with me. After her supper and a little play with my best doll dishes Jessie and I gave Frankie a nice warm bath (her head and all) and put on her clean made-over nightie. Then we sat down on the sofa and had Frankie kneel down by our knees for we are both mothers to her and we taught her to say "Jesus tender Shepherd hear me." She is a very smart child and learned the prayer in no time. Then because Jessie isnt nearly as tall and large as I am, I took Frankie on my lap and rocked her while Jessie told her so sweetly about being God's little girl. She put her poor little boney arm about my neck and snuggled up like a kitten. Mama came in pretty quick and said "Why the child is fast asleep." Auntie let us have a feather bed on a quilt on the floor back of our big bed and Mama helped me e-a-s-e her onto her pillow gently. Jessie and I both spoke of it before we went to sleap how sort of light and yet *big* our harts felt. We love being mothers!...If any thing should happen so Jessie and I didnt marry and have a family we would then be Matron and assistent Matron of an Orphen Assilum. She and I have been onley children to our Mamas so long-- and we *dont believe* in *just one child*.

August 1

Our dear little Frankie has a temper and got naughty in school and wouldnt read her "Is it an ox? Is it an ox" for Miss King. Miss King is very gentle and only had her stand in the corner for ten minutes. Frankie was still pouty and cross at noon time and Jessie and I realized she must be punished. Our mothers never would stand any thing like that from us. First we gave her part of our lunch as we always do. (If you could see the dry bread and stuff the poor child brings in her little rusty pale.!) and then we said solemly "Come Frankie!" and went to Hopkins Woods. Then I said "Frankie you know Jessie and I have adopted you. Do you like being our little girl?" "Uh Huh!" said Frankie still scowling. I went on. "We have been just as nice and loveing to you as our Mamas are to us and we love you dearly but you were very naughty this morning and now we must punish our own child." I dont believe she knew what the word meant but we showed her. I took her across my knees--(just as Jessie and I *both* can remember) and then Jessie *spatted her hard.* (We devide all the care of Frankie.) We both trembled and of course Frankie howled. How it hurts mothers to have to punish their child.! Then I turned her over and cuddled her close and Jessie wiped her tears away and we both told her it hurt us just as bad--and she promised to be a good girl *always.* We kissed her and smoothed her hair and gave her an extra piece of jelly cake we had saved for this and told her jolly stories til she was all happy again. We got back to school just before the bell rang. We felt satisfied but tiard. Frankie was like an angle this afternoon.

April 10, 1877

I want to run a mile tonight just as tight as I can go. Preston is quite a little city and one must keep so proper and not romp much or you'll be called a Tomboy. Its aw-

ful how ladylike a thirteen year old girl must be! Of
course I have good manners (Mama would see to that) but
I get so full of spirits and just joy being alive and I had
most nine years in the free beautiful country where I was
expected to race around to help to make me strong--and
its such a change! I get to feeling like a colt that has
been shut up in the barn all winter. If it wasnt for the
twins and all the fun we have around the house I think Ide
blow up some day. Mama so wishes there was a gymna-
sium in Preston, I suppose if there was they would keep
it just for the boys any how! Mama is going to get me
some dumb bells and maybe the twins can have them too
then she will show us some of the exercises they had in
Papa's school.

April 11

Oh I am so discouraged about ever being any good!
Nell and I exploded this afternoon and cut school and played
we were Gypsies and went along with the river. Then we
came home and I LIED to Mama about it. Arnt you ashamed
to belong to such a girl Journal? I really need to be a
little sick. I am so full of wellness it gets me into scrapes.
Now I have 'fessed all up and cried my eyes out and cant
go to supper (to have Edward and all the rest see what a
sight I am--I couldnt swallow any way--there is such a
lump in my throat) and Ill write you about it not to hear
the dishes click while every body is eating. I am getting
hungry fast. Nellie owned right up when her mother asked
her--got her ears boxed and had an awful scolding (Mrs
Anderson manages differently from Mama) but now I hear
her laughing and jolly. The LIE made all the differance.

I so admire Nellie. She has a quick temper and she is dreadful when she is mad but she wouldn't *sneak*, Katharine Gray. Oh I hate myself Journal! My tongue gets me into scrapes. You see it was the first *real* Spring day--Oh so *lovely* out of doors and we *had* to go to see the Freshit (they think the big brige will go) and of course the twins had to take their music lesson tonight after school so we couldn't go then, for its the other end of town quite a ways. Mary had to go early to school--she is "below" in arithmetic this week and that left Nell and me to get into mischief. Mama says Mary is the *ballance wheal* of the twins. We were trying to think how we would manage to see the river before it calms down and I said to Nellie "Lets go quick this noon--we can run a little on the side streats and go there and back to school and not be *very* late." But Journal we stayed too long. It was such a grand sight-- and then I guess we got to feeling like the river and got a little crazy with the Spring time.

Theres a country road along side that leads to the lake and Nell and I took hold of hands and raced with the river. Oh it was fun! But then we heard the two-forty train whistle. We couldnt *believe* it was so late--but it was. Then as we scrabbled along--hurrying back--I slipped and turned my ancle. Then we *had* to go slow. My it hurt! It does yet and its swelled but I dont mean to worry Mama about it--shes had enough trouble with me this bad day. It was just about four when we got home and Mama was in her room lying down. I couldnt stay away from her another minute and peaped in and she called me.

She said "I missed my girl's goodbye this noon and then I saw that you hadnt taken your history and wondered

how you would manage." Mama looked very pale and tired
and I thought I couldn't own up just then. So I said non-
shalantly, --"Oh that was all right. I borrowed Jennies."
(Jennie May's my seat mate.) See that Journal? First
run away from school--like a kid--then fib about it to ones
dearie Mama!!!!

Mama closed her eyes and looked more tiard.

After a while (I expect she was praying) she said, "Get
the little stool and come close to me Kathie." Then she
talked to me--and it broke my heart all up in little bits
of peaces. As *bad* as I was fealing I was *adoring* Mama--
and admiring the way she did it and thinking if I ever had
a bad girl I would remember not to scold. A solem dignaty
works so much better and is so much more *becoming*.
Mama looked like a sweet angle from Heaven!

It seems Mrs. Anderson thought it was a lovely afternoon to take a drive and asked Mama to go and then they
just rode by the school to leave my history and they thought
they would surprize we girls--hearing a class. Nellie and
I surprized them! (Ho Hum! I'me hungry and making lots
of mistakes.) I never felt so mean inside my heart as I
have this afternoon and then Mama made me feal a worse
sinner by not punishing me any way at all.

I guess Ive got to stop and put some arneca on my ancle
or I cant walk a bit by morning. Oh breakfast seems *so*
far away.

Later--O joy! Nellie just slipped in and brought me a bun
and an orange and a piece of cake. We agreed we would
never cut school again. Nell is awfully sorry too.

Sunday

Journal I have got to be an old maid!! Yes--sad as that will be Ive made up my mind this afternoon and so has Sunny and its all down in two big family Bibles and signed and witnessed by Sunny and me. Oh its terrible what Saint Paul expected of us wimmen!

Sunny and I were getting our Sabath school lesson for next Sunday and as we looked up refrences we came to some awful commands--"Wives submit yourselves unto your Husbands *as unto the Lord*!!" "But I suffer not a woman to teach a man--but be silent!!" "The man is to rule the woman." "Woman was created for the man" and a lot more stuff! Now Journal no one but a Namby Pamby could stand for that! Sunny and I got so excited. How I needed Mama to straighten things out. We just *raved*. Then we got the Bibles and I wrote in ours in the Family Record where a space is left for marages of the children. This is it.

A BLANK FOREVER!!!

This space left a blank for the marriages of the children of Richard and Susan Gray shall never be filled! This is solemly resolved by Katharine E Gray, only surviving child of the above parties.

Signed--Katharine E Gray.
Haven, Aug. 4, 1877

Witnessed by Sunny Osburn.

Now isnt that very *legel* sounding? Sunny fixed her Bible the same. I just had to show mine to somebody. I was so stired up, and Annie was the only one here. I might have known better for she laughed as though she

would have a fit. Then she said "Well Kathie that won't
be binding for you wrote it with a led pencil and only had
one witness." Huh!

Sunday, August 11
    Journal, Jessie and I are going to be Authers! We
are going to "colaberate" and write our first books together. Isnt that a glorious union for us two most *special*
friends? We are each telling our Journals--then we'll
begin.

Monday, August 12
    Gracious me, Journal! My goodness!! Mama doesn't
approve at all of slang but then *she* is a naturel born Spel-
ler. Oh dear! How am I going to be an auther and
thumb the dictionary all the while looking up the right
spelling? We girls have an elegant plot. We just got
that worked out yesterday. Oh its scrumptious! And what
"He says" and "She says" comes so easy to me. I wrote
my first chapter today seventeen minutes quicker than
Jessie did hers but hers was spelled just *beautifully*. I
wanted to duck under the table when my colaberator looked
over my work. She is so patient and so *just* and she didnt
laugh either but *loved* the way I made folks talk, but I
could see that she was dreadfully worried about the spelling as she marked most of the lines. All my paper bags
wasted! I dont know where Ill colect my writing paper
for tomorrow, being away from home. Foolscap costs so
and I didnt bring much money, and I cant borrow of Allie
for our Book is a great secret.

Tuesday

Well Journal I'm in for it! I have begun with the A's in the Dictionary and I plan to go right through learning every word in the book. Its a great responsibility being an Author (Notice that o in Author?) I haven't got to the B's yet.

Haven, Jan 19, 1878

My fourteenth birthday! Two years since I began keeping a diary and I havnt written a word since August. So much has happened I am sure I dont know where to begin. We didnt go back to Preston because Mama couldnt leave Auntie and I began school at the Union Accademy here, going with Sunny. I just love it! Mr Dean is the most wonderful teacher--he is the principal and started the "honor system" when he first came. He made it *impossible* to cheat, makes it easier to be good and some way just knows our natures and helps us get hold of our better selves. Then the boys and girls are such a jolly friendly set and we have the best times, we class mates, all but Harry Rand he is the glumest person I ever saw.

He sits just across the isle from me and never speaks to any one of us and glowers at everything but Mr Dean. Of course I havent been introduced to him. Its too bad he is that kind. His sister Bessie is a dear,--one of my best friends--and his Mother is a lovely lady--Mama knew her long ago.

Haven--Jan 23, 1878

Bessie Rand came home from school with me tonight and Annie got us such a nice tea and Allie played dominoes

with us and sang us some jolly new glees.... On the road
home Bessie said something about her brother Harry and
then I up and asked her what ever made that young person
look so solumn--as though he had lost his last friend,
That was a polite way to put it. He really looks as *cross
as two sticks*. My! I am glad hes not my brother. Then
Bessie said, "I guess that is just it, that he feels no one
likes him or trusts him but his home folks." She says her
mother is anxious about him. All he seems to care about
is his beautiful drawing or to take his dog and gun and go
off in the woods hunting--outside of school that is. He is
very smart and easily at the head of his class. He is a
little older than most of us. He got kept back because of
a dreadful accident the summer before Mr Dean came to
Union a year and a half ago. His horse threw him and ran
away. It was the first time he rode the new horse and he
was a vishious brute, they got rid of right off. Harry's
leg was broken in two places and he was hurt other ways
and couldn't come back to school for more than six months.
By that time Mr Dean had changed things wonderfully. I
dont know quite how he did it--but no one thought of cheating
the least bit any more. To sneak is almost as bad as murder you would think to hear Mr Dean talk in his quiet earnest voice. Well Harry had missed all that "getting into
a straight line" drill those first months and he is proud of
his drawing and always carried a small pocket ruler and
he used it that first day in our awful "free hand" exercise
when we "train our eye" and mustnt measure at all.

Mr Dean said "This is free hand drawing Harry. No
measuring!" But he did it once or twice afterwards. Bessie thought it was force of habit. When his book was full

and handed in Harry got far and away the highest mark and those who had seen him cheat that time were furious but of course they wouldnt tell tails. They werent the class mates he had come up with. He had to go with the B's (having missed so much A work.) He felt *superior* and that didnt help him any. Its gone from bad to worse now. Those who knew and liked him all the way up from the Primary are graduated and gone. Those who saw him cheat (only his first day back Bessie insists) are down on him for keeps and so he gets gloomier and crosser right along.

February 11

This morning most of our class were standing around as usual before the bell rang talking over Lou Hardy's party last night-- and laughing and joking--all of course but Harry Rand. He was in his seat drawing and looking as glum as usual. He is never invited to any of the class parties. In the opening exercises Mr Dean chose "What a Friend We Have in Jesus" and when we came to the words "Do your friends despise--forsake you, Is there trouble any where" Harry stopped singing. His voice is changing and it cracks so I noticed the silence across the isle. I glanced at him out of the corner of my eye. He was scowling harder than ever but someway he looked so *hurt* too and as though he could hardly hold in--as though he wanted to bolt to the barn and ball. In a minute as we got our books out I accidentally (?) dropped my silver pencil which rolled nearly to his seat. He stooped to pick it up (he always *goes through the motions* of being polite) and I stooped too, and our heads bumped together quite hard. (*That* part I *didnt* plan.) I laughed (silently)

and blushed my becomingest and will you believe it--that
misanthrope smiled! Smiled like a sunburst diamond! Why
he is very good looking when he doesnt act the part of
the heavy villain in the play.

I took it we were introduced after that and at noon as
I noticed the far famed drawing book of his on his desk,
I stopped and said "Have you finished that last model Harry? I think its dreadfully hard. " "Why yes, " he answered
real eagerly (such a change to have one of the class girls
speak to him I suppose). Really it was wonderful--rather
better than the printed design. I couldnt have helped prai-
sing it if I had wanted to--and I asked to see the whole
book. I was surprised that any one in Union could do such
work. I nearly wore out my adjectives saying so. The
poor fellows fingers shook as he turned the pages. My!
how ostrachsized he has been feeling. I chanced to look
up and Mr Dean was smiling down at us. He gave me a
quick nod and I knew he approved some of my impulsive
doings.

When I was putting on my wraps I heard Harry Rand
actually whistling. Sunny, Mame and Sue were waiting
for me in the dressing room--and Sue began to scold "Why
Katharine Gray I dont know but that you have spoiled your
chance of being chosen for one of our Class Officers!"
she stormed. "The idea of your speaking to that stuck
up Grumpy--who cheats too! " This made me cross and I
told my dear Susan a few things about this being a free
country. I told her too that I had been watching out a-
cross the isle for a long time and had about made up my
mind that we of Class A were a cruel set of Pharasees!
Granted that he was seen cheating one day--long ago--no

one had ever told me that he did it again. And I said did she think we could reform a sinner by slowly freezing him to death? I reminded her that Bessie Rand was one of our sweetest girls... and that she was worried about her brother and that I for one was through treating him so high and mighty unless he should be bad again. We had quite a little spat but kissed and made up afterwards. I am glad I spoke to him. I am glad I stood up for him and I dont care so awfully to be elected to a class office any way.

April 8

Oh I had a splendid chance to say "I told you so" to Sue and the rest who have criticised Harry Rand and have only just *begun* to speak to him. He helped his sister bring in the trays of the refreshments. We had sand-witches and whipped cream in cocoa and delicious teacakes Bessie frosted her self. Harry was at ease... and was as pleasant as if he hadn't been snubbed to the limit in school circles for a year and a half! When I told Mama she said "He is a carefully trained boy and was acting the polite host to his sister's company." It was a hard place though and I was proud of my protege. He saw me, alone just long enough to ask if he could "come up to Mrs Chases with Bessie some evening" to see me. Oh I am pleased! Mama and Allie both say it will be all right "for Bessie and her Brother to come up". Ahem! Hum! Isnt that sort of *grown uppy* and jolly?

Saturday

Harry and Bessie came up right after supper and we

did have a jolly time! George said "Lets play Jenkins says thumbs up." So we got around the big table and what sport it was! Then we tried Breath Lift and might have broken George's neck when Bessie laughed and lost her breath if Harry hadn't eased him down. The person to be lifted sits with his knees close together and his elbows close to his side (his fingers locked together across his "tummy") Then four people take deep full breaths-- and he must breathe too--all together--and everybody concentrates on the thought they are going to lift the victim on their two fore fingers and find him light as air. At the third breath when every body's lungs are full and their courage good the two on each side slip their two fingertips under the victims arms and knees (held stiff) and *all still holding their breath--lift together.*

Its really wonderful how it can be done. It makes one feel real *spookey.* George was game and so was Harry--and it worked so well and we had so much fun that I ran out on the porch and "Hoo-a-Hoo-d" until Sunny heard and I asked her and Fred to come over. They were as amazed as we had been at first--for they had never tried Breath Lift. It was half past ten before any body thought to look. Harry apologized for staying so late saying he hadnt had such a good time in two years. Everybody liked everybody and it was a first rate little party.

June 20

The grandest thing is going to happen when the five-thirty train comes in to night. *Jessie* is coming to my graduating exercises. Jubilate! Isnt that glorious?

Morning of THE GREAT DAY

Its glorious to have Jessie here. I believe we are going right on being closest, best friends until we are a hundred. She met most all the class last evening and I could see she "took" with them famously. Harry Rand did the most thoughtful thing. Yesterday when he was up Allie was bemoaning that her rose bushes were just little twigs and saying that it was hard to wait for her favorite flower. Right after supper Harry appeared with a big basket full of the most beautiful roses for her, he had picked himself. The Rand's old fashioned garden grows every kind. Harry arranged them so artistically in the basket. He had picked them *with long stems* too. Isnt that unheard of for a boy? Our whole house is as sweet as a fairy bower this morning. Just as he was going he said in a low voice to me "Wear some of the half opened buds for Graduation, Kathie. *Wear* them for me. " Now why should just a nice neighborly word make me blush? Of course I promised and Allie selected some of the nicest buds and Mama pinned them on just now. They set off my plain pretty gown wonderfully. I am so happy wearing them for the class mate who is so changed from the silent gloomy misanthrope to a natural jolly boy.

Late in June-- 1878

I have no business at all to be writing but I am so restless, so full of all that has happened that I just must try it. I am going to Uncle Doctor's tomorrow and believe that he will help my poor hurt eye which is bandaged tight now--so--here goes. I wonder if it is possible for me to be brief--"concise" in any thing I write in my Diary?

Oh the graduation exercises were perfectly lovely in

every respect--dress, music, flowers--(I have told you already that I wore the rose buds that Harry brought) and dear Mr Dean made a splendid address. Mama wiped her eyes twice.

It was great to have Jessie here then and she has been such a comfort since the accident. She is going with us to the City and then home tomorrow. She has stayed so close to me since my eye was hurt--the sweet child!

Our class picnic came two days after graduation. We went in a big coach--everybody--including Mr and Mrs Dean *and* the Blessed Babe who was the happiest of the lot. It had rained and rained lately but the picnic day was ideal. It is such a pretty grove where the river is wide and picturesque. Of course the boats were the big attraction but the river is so high and the current so strong in the middle that Mr Dean used every precaution and only let us go in small numbers with the oldest, strongest boys--and every body had to promise to keep very near shore. Oh, it was beautiful!

Harry took Jessie, Sue and me out and as I have good muscles (thanks to Tom boy days in Menton) I "manned" one pair of oars. I am thankful to say the oars were fastened to the oar locks (or something)--any way they wouldnt get lost and float down stream. Jessie was in the bow, Susie in the stern and of course Harry and I in the center of the boat pulling together just finely.

We were all so happy and Sue especially full of the Dickens. I never saw her look prettier. She wore a white dress with her shade hat tied with blue ribbons and this was pushed off her curls where it did not do a bit of good but just looked picturesque. Why should she care if her nose got freckled on this great day of the class picnic!

Presently Sue spied a tree still in blossom--Its been such a late spring. It was growing well down on a steep bank with long branches reaching out over the river. She said she *must* have some of those flowers and Harry got out his knife and cut her several sprays (while I had hard work to keep our craft steady). Then he dropped the knife, still open, in the bottom of the boat. Enjoying the sweet blossoms, which had waited for us beyond their season, we were about to "pull away." "Oh I *must* have that lovely branch," Sue said, standing right up on the seat, so daringly, and reaching for it. She never was afraid of any thing and that day she was just excited enough to take chances. "Sit Down!" Harry commanded, realizing the danger. He was Captain,--we were trusted to his care and he had a right to give orders--but that was the wrong course to take with pretty, wilful Sue.

She made a saucy face at Harry, sticking out her tongue at him, (looking so cunning) and then she *"lunged"* for that branch! She caught it but lost her ballance and went over board into deep water. Oh the horror of that moment! The branch released as she fell whipped back across the boat tearing my face and--I dont know yet what it did to my eye. Then Jessie was crying out distractedly "Oh she doesnt come up! Why doesnt she come up?" and Harry pulling with all his might to get back out of the grip of the current was saying in quick gasps--"Kathie!--Turn toward me.--Drop your oars.--Take the knife and slit my shoe lacings. There!"--(as I did and he kicked them off) "What possessed me to wear those pesky heavy things?" Then he jerked off his coat and laid it in my lap. A drop of

blood from my cut face fell on his hand. He looked up
anxiously, "Oh you poor girl!" he said--seeing what had
happened--"Can you hold the boat steady? Can you *see*?
Oh I am so sorry about your eye! There, that's just right
for me to dive. I am afraid she has struck her head on
a rock and that is why she doesn't rise. Both of you yell
for help."

Then he went over the side of the boat. Its called a
treacherous river for swimming--the banks are so steep
most places--and there are so many sunken rocks and deep
holes. As he went down I thought of his weakened leg--
mended in two places. Could he succeed in getting poor
Sue? Then we shouted "Help!" and prayed hard in our
hearts. That fraction of time seemed ages--then Harry was
up making a big effort, holding little Sue in one arm. There
was a gash just above her temple and except that the blood
from it flowed, she seemed already dead. Oh how my
heart ached--worse than my eye! I was so proud of Harry
too and praying, *praying* for them both. It took every ounce
of strength I had to hold the boat steady--just out of the
swift current--but Jessie saw what to do--crept forward--
and between the two of them they got the poor girl into the
boat. Then Harry swam, pulling the boat to help me.

I suppose it wasnt a minute until the others came and
soon we were at the landing place. Then began a tremendous effort to revive Sue. Mr Dean was perfectly calm and
splendidly expert and our class "Odd Stick"--Dave Meyers--
distinguished himself. You would think he rescued near-
drowned people once a week. Fortunately a good Doctor
lived close by and was "in" and they got him there to help.

Oh when dear Sue's lids fluttered open and her pretty

blue eyes looked up at us, puzzled but *sane,* in spite of that awful blow on her head--Oh I just dropped where I stood and cried and cried! Jessie was by me in an instant, cuddling my face in her lap and Harry was holding my hand in his, so cold and shakey, and patting my hair and telling me that it was I who saved Sue. "If you hadnt been so strong and steady with the boat, ignoring your own pain-- I couldnt have done a thing" he said tremulously. The idea! Passing the credit on to me after what he dared.

Then the doctor looked Harry and me over--ordered a hot drink for him and dry clothes--then home as soon as possible and to bed. The Wentworth Grove folks were eager to help and carried him off--escorted by several of the class boys. Then the Doctor pryed the lid of my eye open (of course it was badly swollen and Oh the light hurt!) and said the sight was safe if I had good care--and he bandaged it for the ride home. Some one loaned a spring wagon, put a mattress on its floor and Sue, wrapped in blankets was tenderly lifted in, her wounded head on a pillow in Mame's lap and most carefully driven home.

Lorenzo who is dignified and steady in an emergency was trusted to ride ahead on a fast horse to break the news to Sue's mother and get their family doctor on the spot, also to call Dr Hodge to go to Allies to treat my eye and to Harry's to make sure he was all right. Soon a very sober and shaken crowd got into the picnic coach and hurried homeward. Mr Dean kept an anxious eye on Harry who still trembled and didn't get his color back. Jessie held a big black umbrella down close over my head to keep the glare of the sun on the sandy road from my eye while Mrs Dean sitting by me on the other side held my hand

and patted it mother fashion. It was a very solemn time for us young folks who had gone out in the morning fairly bursting with high spirits. In the midst of the gayety we had come "in the twinkling of an eye" very, very close to grim Death.

At last Dave Meyers tilted that expressive foot of his upon end (I didnt see--Jessie told me afterward, so amused) and folding all but two fingers of his right hand tapped the palm of his left one. We knew then that "A burst of eloquence"--as the books remark--was getting under way. He began:--"We deeply regret that we have long misjudged the Hero in our midst. I speak of our class mate and brother Harold Rand." "Cut that out Dave," growled Harry so embarrassed, "Here! Here!" the crowd shouted, approving Dave. "A tardy acknowledgment at best, Harold," Dave continued elegantly. "A word fitly spoken, Dave" said Mr Dean so heartily. Then little Eddie Boswell--"the Kid of the Klass"--hopped up swinging his cap and crying "Three cheers for our class Hero who forgot his mended leg and weighed down by heavy clothes dove into the deep water to save a drowning girl--and three cheers for the class Heroine who helped him so pluckily if her eye was busted!" Every body laughed shakily at that and gave choken cheers over and over, while Harry and I protested "it was nothing at all" and got redder and redder. So we drove up to Allie's.

A Suburb of Haven

The Last of July--1878

Dates are no consequence this summer for the days are pretty much alike. We are just back from Uncle Doctors after a horrid month. I am limited to ten minutes use of my well eye a day, with the sick one barricaded behind a green silk shade. It isnt exactly *festive*, Journal dear. But though the accident to my eye proved more serious than we thought at first, its doing quite well. When Uncle first saw it he said "My patience! That looks like raw beef" and hurried me to a very fine doctor who just treats eyes. The Eye ball was swolen even with my brow and was very, very painful. I am not going to think any more about those days. Its too harrowing. Times up!

Next day.

Mama and I are boarding at Uncle George's in the "real regular" country, about three miles from Haven. The air here is supposed to be "extra special" for a girl who is pretty white and peaked after weeks in a dark room. I cant say I am "bubbling over with enthusiasm" to be clear away from the girls and our crowd--but then I couldn't do any thing to have any fun, anyway. I get out a little, under the big trees on cloudy days--and am promised a ride in the twilight tonight with "old Jake" when he takes the great cans of milk to the cheese factory. Jake has worked for Uncle George since he was a young boy and is a character. He sits out by the back door every evening and plays the accordian, choosing very mournful tunes which make Towser howl. So cheerful! Any way I found a nest of kittens in the barn last twilight (when I take my walks) and Mama reads to me by the hour and we play dominoes and parchesi. It isnt easy you know--even with every one so kind-- but it takes time to cure a scratched eye ball and I've just got to be patient. My face or eyelid are not scarred at all.

August 10.

Well its going better! Sue *walked* all the way out here
one day--and begged a ride another--to come and read a
jolly book aloud to me. The poor child feels so guilty
about my eye! She is well as ever again and just does her
hair another way--even more becoming--to hide that scar.
I have lovely letters from the class girls who are away
and of course from Allie and my Jessie. Harry writes too.
Mama says they are "fine, boyish letters". Ill 'fess I
didnt show her the last one. It wasnt "mushy" at all, Jour-
nal--but I felt sort of shy about it. He wrote so sympa-
thisingly about my eye and signed himself "Your Stronghold".
I like that name and it sutes Harry. He will be in Michi-
gan until September. My eye is much stronger but I am
afraid there will be no school for me this fall.

Hill Top Home--(Allie's)
Thanksgiving Day--1878

I never had such a thankful Thanksgiving Day in my
life! The old green shade is tucked way back in a bureau
drawer and I can go out the sunniest days wearing cute blue
glasses ("nose-grabbers" not specs) which are very becoming only I mustnt smile broadly, with them on, for my
cheeks *rise up* and push them off--to dangle on the cord.
(Some twisted sentence that but never mind!) I am *back in*
school with our own beloved crowd! After weeks and weeks
in a dark room,--can you beat that for blessedness?

The last week in August Mr Dean got back and came
to see us. I had just got home from the oculists feeling
very much encouraged. Mr Dean urged me to come into
the "Advanced Class" for part time work as soon as it was

safe for me to be in broad daylight,--said I learned readily
and would get much from just listening to recitations and
that he knew he could promise every one would "lend their
eyes" to help me study.   With this hope it was surprising
how fast I gained and I did go the very first day, wearing
my shade.   There was a near riot to have the "Honor"(!)
of "learning lessons for Kathie"--(and by the way I was not
the only one helped.   All that extra going over things "set"
the subjects in my "Conductors" minds) Sue took the Latin
as her special field saying any body with half an eye could
see she had best rights.   Many a happy hour we have spent
in the cloak room buzzing away at vocabularies and conju-
gations.   Harry can explain Algebra so even my wooden head
can see some sense in A + Y = X etc.   We have the school
library for the tutoring for one period every day.   *Honest*
and truly we play fair!--Ill enclose a report card to prove
it.   We *never* stop "boneing" til the bell rings. ("Hardly
ever"!)

Were there ever such loyal classmates? I adore them
all!   I have hardly needed my eyes this fall but to enjoy
the scenery and beam affection on my Helpers.   Of course
I have to be very careful and cant talk with you often, old
Dear.

Gretchen was eleven when she began her diary in Vienna. Precocious and inordinately curious, she used her diary to record what she was learning about the facts of life, some of those "facts" being heretofore unknown to us all.

She had an older sister, Dora, who could have educated her about the birds and the bees, but Gretchen, like many a girl, didn't get along well with her sister and, therefore, was not privy to her stock of information. Her best friend, Hella, became Gretchen's chief informer and confidante — the two of them putting their heads together in "sexual research."

Sigmund Freud happened upon Gretchen's diary and was instrumental in having it published. In an introduction he wrote for the book he called it a "gem" which would be a classic portrait of adolescence. The book has long been studied by psychologists, but has never really received its deserved attention among those who would be most interested in Gretchen's research, young girls with a similar curiosity.

"Gretchen Lainer" was a pseudonym used to protect the identity of the actual young girl who wrote the diary. She wrote this early in the 1900's but the exact dates of her birth and death are unknown.

Gretchen Lainer

July 12, 19...

Hella and I are writing a diary. We both agreed that when we went to the high school we would write a diary every day. Dora keeps a diary too, but she gets furious if I look at it. I call Helene "Hella," and she calls me "Rita"; Helene and Grete are so vulgar. Dora says little children (she means me and Hella) ought not to keep a diary. She says they will write such a lot of nonsense. No more than in hers.

July 25

I've had a frightful row with Dora. She says I've been fiddling with her things. It's all because she's so untidy. As if her things could interest me. Yesterday she left her letter to Erika lying about on the table, and all I read was: He's as handsome as a Greek god. I dont know who "he"

71

was for she came in at that moment. It's probably Krail
Rudi, with whom she is everlastingly playing tennis and
carries on like anything. As for handsome--well, there's
no accounting for tastes.

July 26

It's a good thing I brought my dolls' portmanteau. Mother said: "You'll be glad to have it on rainy days. Of
course I'm much too old to play with dolls, but even though
I'm 11 I can make dolls' clothes still. One learns something while one is doing it, and when I've finished something
I do enjoy it so. Mother cut me out some things and I was
tacking them together. Then Dora came into the room and
said: Hullo, the child is sewing things for her dolls. What
cheek, as if she had never played with dolls. Besides, I
don't really play with dolls any longer. When she sat down
beside me I sewed so vigorously that I made a great scratch
on her hand, and said: Oh, I'm so sorry, but you came too
close. I hope she'll know why I really did it. Of course
she'll go and sneak to Mother. Let her. What right has
she to call me child. She's got a fine red scratch anyhow,
and on her right hand where everyone can see.

July 30

Today is my birthday. Father gave me a splendid
parasol with a flowered border and painting materials and
Mother gave me a huge postcard album for 800 cards. It
is glorious to have a birthday, everyone is so kind, even
Dora.

July 31

Yesterday was heavenly. We laughed till our sides

ached over Consequences. I was always being coupled with Robert and oh the things we did together, not really of course but only in writing: kissed, hugged lost in the forest, bathed together; but I say I wouldn't do *that* ! That won't happen, it's quite impossible!

August 3

I got a chill bathing the other day so now I am not allowed to bathe for a few days. Robert keeps me company. We are quite alone and he tells me all sorts of tales.

August 12

They have a society called T. Au. M. , that is in Latin Be Silent or Die in initial letters. No one may betray the society's secrets, and when they make a new member he has to strip off all his clothes and lie down naked and every one spits on his chest and rubs it and says: Be One of Us, but all in Latin. Then he has to go to the eldest and biggest who gives him two or three cuts with a cane and he has to swear that he will never betray anyone. Then everyone smokes a cigarette and touches him with the lighted end on the arm or somewhere and says: Every act of treachery will burn you like that. And then the eldest, who has a special name which I can't remember, tattoos on him the word Taum, that is Be Silent or Die, and a heart with the name of a girl. Robert says that if he had known me sooner he would have chosen "Gretchen." I asked him what name he had tattooed on him, but he said he was not allowed to tell. I shall tell Oswald to look when they are bathing and to tell me. He said there was a lot more which he couldn't tell me because it's too tremendous.

Then I had to swear that I would never tell anyone about the society and he wanted me to take the oath upon my knees, but I wouldn't do that and he nearly forced me to my knees. In the end I had to give him my hand on it and a kiss. I didn't mind giving him that, for a kiss is nothing, but nothing would induce me to kneel down. Still, I was in an awful fright, for we were quite alone in the garden and he took me by the throat and tried to force me to my knees. All that about the *society* he told me when we were quite alone for he said: I can't have your name tattooed on me because it's against our laws to have two names but now that you have sworn I can let you know what I really am and think in secret.

I couldn't sleep all night for I kept on dreaming of the society, wondering whether there are such societies in the high school and whether Dora is in a society and has a name tattooed on her. But it would be horrible to have to strip naked before all one's schoolfellows. Perhaps in the societies of the high school girls that part is left out. But I shouldn't like to say for sure whether I'd have Robert's name tattooed on me.

September 3

Such a horrid thing has happened. I shall never speak to R. again. It was frightful cheek of him to tickle me as he did, and I gave him such a kick. I think it was on his nose or his mouth. Then he actually dared to say: After all I'm well paid out, for what can one expect when one keeps company with such young monkeys, with such babies. Fine talk from him when he's not 14 himself yet. It was all humbug about his being 15 and he seems to be one of the idlest boys in the school, never anything but Satisfactory in his reports, and he's not in the fifth yet, but only in the fourth. Anyhow, we've settled our accounts. Cheeky devil.

October 4

Oswald cant go back to S. He has been up to something, I wish I knew what, perhaps something in the closet. He always stays there such a long time. I noticed that when I was in the country. Or perhaps it may have been something in his society. Father is furious and Mother's eyes are all red with crying. At dinner nobody says a word. If I could only find out what he's done. Father was shouting at him yesterday and both Dora and I heard what he said: You young scamp (then there was something we couldn't understand) and then he said, you attend to your school books and leave the girls and the married women alone you pitiful scoundrel. And Dora said: Ah, now I understand and I said: Please tell me, he is my brother as well as yours. But she said: "You wouldn't understand. It's not suitable for such young ears." Fancy that, it's suitable for her ears, but not mine though she's not quite three years older than I am, but because she no longer wears a short skirt she gives herself the airs of a grown-up *lady*. Such airs, and then she sneaks a great spoonful of jam so that her mouth is stuffed with it and she can't speak. Whenever I see her do this, I make a point of speaking to her so that she has to answer.

October 9

I know all about it now!!! That's how babies come. And *that* is what Robert really meant. Not for me, thank

you, I simply won't marry. For if one marries one has
to do it; it hurts frightfully and yet one has to. What a
good thing that I know it in time. But I wish I knew exactly how. It lasts nine months till the baby comes and
then a lot of women die. It's horrible. Hella has known
it for a long time but didn't like to tell me. A girl told
her last summer in the country. She wanted to talk about
it to Lizzi her sister, really she only wanted to ask if it
was all true and Lizzi ran off to her mother to tell her
what Hella had said. And her mother said: "These children
are awful, a corrupt generation, don't you dare to repeat
it to any other girl, to Grete Lainer, for instance," and
she gave her a box on the ear. As if she could help it!
That is why she didn't write to me for such a long time.
Poor thing, poor thing, but now she can tell all about it
and we won't betray one another. My goodness, how curious
I am to know.

October 10

I thought I knew all about it but only now has Hella
really told me everything. It's a horrible business this...
I really can't write it. She says that of course Inspee has
it already, had it when I wrote that Inspee wouldn't bathe,
did not want to bathe; really she had *it*. Whatever happens
one must always be anxious about it. *Streams of blood*
says Hella. But then everything gets all bl... That's why
in the country Inspee always switched off the light before
she was quite undressed, so that I couldn't see. Ugh!
Catch me looking! It begins at 14 and goes on for 20 years
or more.

October 21

Berta Franke says that when one is dark under the eyes one has *it* and that when one gets a baby then one doesn't have it any more until one gets another. She told us too how one gets it, but I didn't really believe what she said, for I thought she did not know herself exactly. Then she got very cross and said: "All right, I wont tell you any more. If I dont know myself." But I cant believe what she said about husband and wife. She said it must happen every night, for if not they don't have a baby. That's why they have their beds so close together. People call them *marriage beds*!!! And it hurts so frightfully that one can hardly bear it. But one has to for a husband can make his wife do it. I should like to know how he can make her. But I didn't dare to ask for I was afraid she would think I was making fun of her. Men have *it* too, but very seldom. We see a lot of Berta Franke now, she is an awfully nice girl, perhaps Mother will let me invite her here next Sunday.

October 27

Everything seems to have gone wrong. Yesterday I got unsatisfactory in history, and in arithmetic today I couldn't get a single sum right.

November 2

I dont know all about things yet. Hella knows a lot more. We said we were going to go over our natural history lesson together and we went into the drawing-room, and there she told me a lot more. Then Mali, our new servant, came in, and she told us something horrid. Mali told us that all the Jews when they are quite little have to go through a very dangerous operation; it hurts frightfully and that's why they are so cruel. It's done so that they can have more children; but only little boys, not the girls. It's horrid, and I should not like to marry a Jew. Then we asked Mali whether it is true that *it* hurts so frightfully and she laughed and said: It can't be so bad as all that, for if it were you wouldn't find everyone doing it. Then Hella asked her: But have you done it already, you haven't got a husband? She said: Go on, Miss! One mustn't ask such questions it's not ladylike. We were in an awful funk, and begged her not to tell Mother. She promised not to.

November 8

There was such a lovely young lady skating today, and she skates so beautifully, inside and outside edge and figures of 8. I skated along behind her. When she went to the cloak room there was such a lovely scent. I wonder if she is going to be married soon and whether *she* knows all about everything. She is so lovely and she pushes back the hair from her forehead so prettily. I wish I were as pretty as she is. But I am dark and she is fair. I wish I could find out her name and where she lives. I must go skating again tomorrow.

November 9

I'm so upset; *she* didn't come to skate. I'm afraid she may be ill.

November 12

She has spoken to me. I was standing near the entrance gate and suddenly I heard some one laughing behind me and I knew directly: That is *she*! So it was. She came up and said: Shall we skate together? Please, if I may, said I, and we went off together crossing arms. My heart was beating furiously, and I wanted to say something, but couldn't think of anything sensible to say. When we came back to the entrance a gentleman stood there and took off his hat and she bowed, and she said to me: Till next time. I said quickly: When? Tomorrow? Perhaps, she called back.... Only perhaps, perhaps, oh I wish it were tomorrow.

November 22

When I was coming away from the religion lesson with Berta Franke the other day, of course we began talking about *it*. She says that's why people marry, only because of it. I said that I could not believe that people marry only for *that*. Lots of people marry and then have no children. That's all right said Berta, but it's quite true what I tell you. Then she told me a lot more but I really can't write it all down. It is too horrid, but I shan't forget.

November 25

I can't manage to go skating every day. I do love the Gold Fairy, that is my name for *her*, for I hate her real name. Inspee declares that they call her Stasi for short, but I dont believe that; most likely they call her Anna, but that's so common. Thank goodness Hella always calls me Rita, so at school I'm known as Rita. It's only at home that they will call me Gretl.

February 20

I met the Gold Fairy today. She spoke to me and asked why I did not come skating any more. I said: Would you believe it, a year ago my sister had an earache, and *for that reason* they won't allow *either* of us to skate this year. She laughed like anything and said so exquisitely: Oh, what a wicked sister. She looked perfectly ravishing: A red-brown coat and skirt trimmed with fur, sable I believe and a huge brown beaver hat with crepe-de-chine ribbons, lovely. And her eyes and mouth. Next autumn, when we get new winter clothes, I shall have a fur trimmed red-brown.

July 24

My birthday is coming soon, thank goodness I shall be 12 then, only 2 years more and I shall be 14; I am so glad.

August 10

I do really think! A boy can always get what he wants. Oswald is really going for a fortnight to Znaim to stay with his chum; only Oswald of course. I should like to see what would happen if Dora or I wanted to go anywhere. A boy has a fine time. It's the injustice of the thing which makes me furious. For we know for certain that he's had a bad report, even though he does not tell us anything about it. But of course that doesn't matter. They throw every 2 in our teeth and when he gets several Satisfactories he can go wherever he likes. His chum too: he only got to know Max Rozny this year and he's a chum already. Hella and I have been chums since we were in the second in the elementary school. We both gave him a piece of our mind about friendship. He laughed scornfully and said:

That's all right, the friendships of *men* become closer as the years pass, but the friendships of you girls go up in smoke as soon as the first admirer turns up. What cheek. Whatever happens Hella and I shall stick to one another till we're married, for we want to be married on the same day. Naturally she will probably get engaged before me but she *must* wait for me before she's married. That's simply her duty as a friend.

August 31

Oswald's having a fine long fortnight; he's still there and can stay till September 4th!! If it had been Dora or me. There would have been a frightful hulabaloo. But Oswald may do *anything*. Ada says: We girls must take for ourselves what the world won't give us of its own free will.

September 25

All the girls are madly in love with Professor Wilke the natural history professor. Hella and I walked behind him today all the way home. He is a splendid looking man, so tall that his head nearly touched the lamp when he stands up quickly, and a splendid fair beard like fire when the sun shines on it; a Sun God! we call him S. G. , but no one knows what it means and who we are talking about.

December 5

Skating today I saw the Gold Fairy. She is awfully pretty, but I really don't think her so lovely as I did last year. Hella says she never could think what had happened to my eyes. "You were madly in love with her and you never noticed that she has a typical Bohemian nose," said

Hella. Of course that's not true, but now my taste is *quite different*.

December 9

It's awful. At 2 o'clock this afternoon Hella was taken to the Löw sanatorium and was operated on at once. Appendicitis. Her mother has just telephoned that the operation has been successful. But the doctors said that 2 hours later it would have been too late. My knees are trembling and my hand shakes as I write.

December 14

This afternoon I was with Hella from two until a 1/4 to 4. She is so pale and when I came in we both cried such a lot. I brought her some more flowers and I told her directly that when he sees me Prof. W. always asks after her. When anyone is lying in bed they look quite different, like strangers. I said so to Hella, and she said: We can never be strangers to one another, not even in death. Then I burst out crying again and both our mothers said I must go away because it was too exciting for Hella.

December 20

I am so glad, tomorrow or Tuesday Hella can come home, in time for the Christmas tree. Now I know what to give her, a long chair, Father will let me, for I have not enough money myself but Father will give me as much as I want. Oh there's no one like Father!

December 21

The couch is lovely, a Turkish pattern with long tassels on the round bolster. Father wanted to pay for it altogether, but I said: No, then it would not be my present, and so I paid five crowns and Father 37. Tomorrow early it will be sent to the Bruckners.

December 23

Hella went home today. Her father carried her upstairs while I held her hand.

December 26

Hella was awfully pleased with the couch, her father carried her into the room and laid her on the sofa. Her mother cried. It was touching. It's certainly awfully nice to have got through a bad illness, when everyone takes care of one, and when no one denies you the first place. I dont grudge it to Hella. She's such a darling.

March 29

Today something horrible happened to Dora and me. I simply can't write it down. She was awfully nice and said: Two years ago on the Metropolitan Railway the same thing had happened when she was travelling with Mother on February 15th. She and Mother were sitting together and a gentleman was standing farther down the carriage where Mother could not see him but Dora could. And as Dora was looking he opened his cloak and -- -- --! just what the man did today at the house door. And when they got out of the train Dora's boa got stuck in the door and she had to turn round though she did not want to, and then she saw again -- -- --! She simply could not sleep for a whole month afterwards. She never told anyone except Erika and the

same thing happened to her once. Dora says that happens
at least once to nearly every girl; and that such men are
"*abnormal.*" I don't really know what that means, but I
did not like to ask. Perhaps Hella will know. Of course
I did not really look, but Dora shivered and said: And *that*
is what one has to endure. And then, when we were talking
it over she said to me that that was why Mother was ill
and because she has had five children. Then I was very
silly and said: "But how from *that*?" One does not get children from that? "Of course," she said "I thought you knew
that already... Then I was silly again, really frightfully
stupid; for instead of telling her what I really knew I said:
"Oh, yes, I knew all about it except just that." Then she
burst out laughing and said: "After all, what you and Hella
know doesn't amount to much." And in the end she told me
a *little*. If it's really as Dora says, then she is right when
she says it is better not to marry. One can fall in love,
one must fall in love, but one can just break off the engagement. Well, that's the best way out of the difficulty
for then no one can say that you've never had a man in love
with you.

On the way home I told Hella the awful thing we'd seen
the man do. She does not know either what "abnormal"
really means as far as this is concerned. But now we shall
use it as an expression for something horrible. Of course
no one will understand us. And then Hella told me about
a drunken man who in Nagy K... was walking through the
streets *like that* and was arrested. She says *too* that one
can never forget seeing anything like *that*. Hella knows
too that it is from that that one gets children. She ex-
plained it all to me and now I can quite understand that

that must make one ill.   Hella says: *That* is the original
sin, and *that* is the sin which Adam and Eve commited.
Before I had always believed that the original sin was something quite different.   But that--that.   Since yesterday I've
been so upset.   I always seem to be seeing *that*; really I
did not look at all, but I must have seen it all the same.

March 30

I don't know why, but in the history lesson today it all
came into my head once more what Dora had said of Father.
But I really can't believe it.   Because of Father I'm really
sorry that I know it.   Perhaps it does not all happen the
way Dora and Hella say.   Generally I can trust Hella, but
of course she may be mistaken.

April 1

Today Dora told me a lot more.   She is quite different
now from what she used to be.   One does not say P(eriod),
but M(enstruation).   Only common people say P--.   Or one
can say one's like that.   Dora has had M-- since August
before last, and it is horribly disagreeable, because men
always know.   That is why at the High School we have only
three men professors and all the other teachers are women.
Now Dora often does not have M-- and then sometimes it's
awfully bad, and that's why she's anemic.   That men always
know, that's frightfully interesting.

April 4

We talk a lot about such things now.   Dora certainly
knows more than I do, that is not more but better.   But
she isn't quite straightforward all the same.   When I asked

her how she got to know about it all, whether Erika told
her or Frieda, she said "Oh, I don't know; one finds it all
out somehow; one need only use one's eyes and one's ears,
and then one can reason things out a little." But seeing
and hearing don't take one very far. I've always kept my
eyes open and I'm not so stupid as all that. One must be
told by some one, one *can't* just happen upon it by oneself.

April 9

Today is Father and Mother's *wedding day*. Now I know
what that really means. Dora says it can't really be true
that it is the most lovely day in one's life, as everyone
says it is, especially the poets.

April 24

We went to confession and communion today. I do hate
confession though it's never happened to me what many girls
have told me, even girls in the Fifth. No priest has ever
asked me about the 6th commandment; all they've asked is:
In thought, word, or deed? Still, I do hate going to confession, and so does Dora. It's much nicer for Hella as a
Protestant for they have no confession. And at communion
I'm always terrified that the host might drop out of my
mouth. That would be awful. I expect one would be immediately excommunicated as a heretic.

April 26

In the Third there really is a girl who dropped the host
out of her mouth. There was a frightful row about it. She
said it was not her fault, the priest's hand shook so. It's
quite true, he was very old, and that is why I'm always

afraid it will happen to me.

June 1

We've had such an experience today! It's awful; it's quite true then that one takes off *every stitch* when one is madly fond of anyone. We've seen it *with our own eyes.* I was just sitting and reading Storm's The Rider of the Grey Horse and Dora was arranging some writing paper to take to Fanzensbad when Resi came and said: Fraulein Dora, please come here a moment, I want you to look at something! From the tone of her voice I saw there was something up so I went too. At first Resi would not say what it was, but Dora was generous and said: "It's all right, you can say everything before her." Then we went into Resi's room and from behind the curtain peeped into the mezzanine. A young *married couple* live there!!! At least Resi says people say they are not really married, but simply live together!!!! And what we saw was awful. She was absolutely naked lying in bed without any of the clothes on, and he was kneeling by the bedside quite n-- too, and he kissed her all over, everywhere!!! Dora said afterwards it made her feel quite sick. And then he stood up and -- no, I can't write it, it's too awful, I shall never forget it. So *that's* the way of it, it's simply frightful. I could never have believed it. Dora went as white as a sheet and trembled so that Resi was terribly frightened. I nearly cried with horror, and yet I could not help laughing too. I was really afraid he would stifle her because he's so big and she's so small. And Resi says he is certainly much too big for her, that he nearly tears her. I don't know why he should tear her but certainly he might have crushed her. Dora was so

terrified she had to sit down and Resi hurried to get her a
glass of water, because she believed she was going to faint.
I had not imagined it was anything like *that*, and Dora certainly had not either.   Or she would never have trembled
so.   Still, I really don't see why she should tremble like
that.   There is no reason to be frightened, one simply need
not marry, and then one need never strip off every stitch,
and oh dear, poor Mademoiselle who is so small and the
lieutenant is very tall.   But just think if anyone is as fat
as Herr Richter or our landlord.   Or course Herr Richter
is at least 50, but last January the landlord had *another*
little girl, so something *must* have happened.   No, I'm sure
it's best not to marry, for *it* is really too awful.   We did
not look any more for then came the worst, suddenly Dora
began to be actually sick, so that she could hardly get back
to our room.   If she had not been able to, everything would
have come out.   Mother sent for the doctor directly and he
said that Dora was very much overworked; that it was a
good thing she was going away from Vienna in a few days.
No girl ought to study, it does not pay.   Then he said to
me: "You don't look up to much either.   What are you so
hollow eyed for?"   "I'm so frightened about Dora," I said.
"Fiddlededee," said the doctor, "that does not give anyone
black rings round the eyes."   So it must be true that one
gets to look ill when one always has to think about *such*
things.

June 3

Father took Hella and me to Kahlenberg; we enjoyed
ourselves tremendously.   After dinner, when Father was
reading the paper in the hotel, we went to pick flowers,

and I told Hella all about what we'd seen on Friday. She was simply speechless, all the more since she had never heard what Mad. told us about taking off everything. She won't marry either, for it's too disagreeable, indeed too horrid. Hella is frightfully annoyed that she was not there. She can be jolly glad, I don't want to see it a second time, and I shall never forget it all my life long; what I saw at the front door was nothing to this.

Dora has just said to me: It's horrible that one has to endure that (you know what!!! -- -- -- --) when one is married. I'm afraid every night that I'm going to dream about it, and Dora has dreamed about it already. She says that whenever she closes her eyes she sees it all as if it were actually before her.

June 4

We understand now *what* Father meant the other day when he was speaking about Dr. Diller and his wife and said: "But they dont suit one another at all." I thought at the time he only meant that it looks so absurd for so tiny a woman to go about with a big strong man. But that's only a minor thing; the main point is something quite different!!!! Hella and I look at all couples now who go by arm in arm, thinking about them from *that* point of view, and it amuses us so much as we are going home that we can hardly keep from laughing. But really it's no laughing matter, especially for the woman.

June 6

What I think worst of all is that one saw the whole of his behind, it was really disgusting. Dora said the other

day she thought it positively infamous. Resi said they might
at least have pulled down the blind so that nobody could see
in, that's what respectable people would do. But *respectable*
people simply would not strip, or at least they'd cover themselves respectably with the bedclothes.

One thing that puzzles me is that I never dream about
it. I should like to know whether perhaps Dora never really dreamed of it, though she pretended she did. As for
Hella saying she dreamed of it the day before yesterday,
I'm sure that was pure invention, for she was not there at
all. She says it's a good thing she was not for if she had
been she would have burst out laughing. But I fancy if she'd
seen what we saw she would have found there was nothing
to laugh at.

June 26

It's really stupid how anxious I am now at Communion
lest the host should drop out of my mouth. I was so anxious I was very nearly sick. Hella says there must be some
reason for it, but I don't know of any, except that the accident which that girl Lutter in the Third had made me even
more anxious than I was before. Hella says I'd better turn
Protestant, but nothing would induce me to do that; for after
Com. one feels so pure and so much better than one was
before. But I'm sorry to say it does not last so long as
it ought to.

October 16

I had a frantically anxious time in the arithmetic lesson
today. All of a sudden Hella flushed dark red and I thought
to myself: Aha, that's it! And I wrote to her on my black-

line paper: Has it begun??? for we had agreed that she would tell me directly, she will be 14 in February and *it* will certainly begin soon. Frau Doktor F. said: Lainer, what was that you pushed over to Br.? and she came up to the desk and took the black-line paper. "What does that mean: Has it begun???" Perhaps she really did not know what I meant, but several of the girls who knew about it too laughed, and I was in a terrible fright. But Hella was splendid. "Excuse me, Frau Doktor, Rita asked whether the frost had begun yet." "And that's the way you spend your time in the mathematics lesson?" But thank goodness that made things all right. Only in the interval Hella said that really I am inconceivably stupid sometimes. What on earth did I want to write a thing like that for? When *it* begins, *of course* she will let me know directly. As a matter of fact it has *not* begun yet. We have agreed now that it will be better to say "Endt," a sort of portmanteau word of developed (entwickelt) and at last (endlich). That will really be splendid and Hella says that I happened upon it in a lucid interval. It's really rather cheeky of her, but after all one can forgive anything to one's friend. She absolutely insists that I must never again put her in such a fix in class. Of course it happened because I am always thinking: Now then, this is the day.

January 5

Most important, Hella since yesterday evening -- -- --! She did not come to school yesterday, for the day before she felt frightfully bad, and her mother really began to think she was going to have another attack of appendicitis. Instead of that!!! She looks so ill and interesting, I spent the whole afternoon and evening with her; and at first she did not want to tell me what was the matter. But when I said I should go away if she did not tell me, she said: "All right, but you must not make such idiotic faces, and above all you must not look at me." "Very well," I said, "I won't look, but tell me everything about it." So then she told me that she had felt frantically bad, as if she was being cut in two, much worse than after the appendicitis operation, and then she had frantically high fever and shivered at the same time, all Friday and yesterday -- -- -- tableau!! And then her mother told her the chief things, though she knew them already. She acted the innocent to her mother, as if she knew nothing at all, and her mother kissed her and said, now you are not a child any more, now you belong among the grown-ups. How absurd, so *I* am still a child! After all, on July 30th I shall be 14 too, and at least one month before I shall have it too, so I shan't be a *child* for more than six months more. Hella and I laughed frightfully, but she is really a little puffed up about it; she won't admit that she is, but I noticed it quite clearly. The only girl I know who did not put on airs when that happened was Ada. Because of the school Hella is awfully shy, and before her father too. But her mother has promised her not to tell him. If only one can trust her!!!

July 2

My goodness, today I have.....,no, I can't write it plain out. In the middle of the Physics lesson, during revision, when I was not thinking of anything in particular, Fraulein N. came in with a paper to be signed. As we all stood up I thought to myself: Hullow, what's that? And then it suddenly occurred to me: Aha!! In the interval Hella asked me why I had got so fiery red in the Physics lesson, if I'd had some sweets with me. I did not want to tell her the real reason directly, and so I said: "Oh no, I had nearly fallen asleep from boredom, and when Fraulein N. came in it gave me a start." On the way home I was very silent, and I walked so slowly (for of course one must not walk fast *when*...) that Hella said: "Look here, what's up today, that you are so frightfully solemn? Have you fallen in love without my knowing it, or is it *at long last*...?" Then I said "Or is it *at long last*!" And she said: "Ah, then now we're equals once more," and there in the middle of the street she gave me a kiss.

Selma Lagerlöf

Just as she planned in this diary written at age fourteen, Selma Lagerlöf became a great writer. In fact, she was the first woman to win the Nobel Prize for Literature. She is most remembered for her fictionalized accounts of her childhood home, Mårbacka, and for her novel, **Gösta Berlings Saga.**

This little-known diary is a record of a winter's stay in Stockholm with her aunt and uncle. She left her family in the country in order to receive daily treatments for a lame leg at a clinic in the city.

Her powerful imagination is what strikes us most here; she took what, on the surface, seems like a rather uneventful stay with relatives and turns it into an unforgettable tale.

1858 - 1940

Selma Lagerlöf

THE JOURNEY TO STOCKHOLM

Monday, January 20, 1873.

On the train from Kil to Laxå.

Elin Laurell gave me a lovely daybook for Christmas. It has a dainty white binding, a blue back and gilt edges, It is such a pretty book it seems almost a pity to write in it.

"But that is just what it's for," Elin said, and that I should accustom myself to jotting down all that happens to me from day to day, as it will be useful to me and a pleasure in afteryears.

I hardly think that I should have kept a diary had I stayed at home, as nothing ever happens in winter at Marbacka. One day is exactly like another. But now that I'm going to Stockholm, I have put the book in my bag and am taking it with me.

The train shakes dreadfully, and my hands are numb with the cold, but I don't mind much. The worst of it is I do not know how one usually writes in a daybook.

Elin Laurell says that if one is to become an author one must be thankful for every experience and glad, too, if one meets with trials that are hard to bear; for otherwise one cannot describe how it feels to be unhappy.

So perhaps I had better jot down what Nurse Maja told me before I left for Stockholm. It may be of use to me when I'm old enough to write novels.

Still, it was a pity, for until then I had been so happy in the thought of the journey. I had fared so well at the home of my uncle five years ago, and the exercises at the Institute had made me well and strong. Anyhow, I am glad to have the company of Daniel on the journey. He is going back to Upsala after the Christmas holidays. Daniel is always kind and considerate, and I think the world of him!

Having to get up at three this morning was not pleasant, but we had to do it in order to arrive at Kil station in time to catch the train for Stockholm. Everyone, except Papa, of course, was up to bid Daniel and me goodbye. I thought they all looked forlorn as they sat round the coffee table, but that was perhaps because they were sleepy and half frozen. I was sleepy and cold, too, but I was happy, and laughed and chattered. Aunt Lovisa remarked that evidently I was not sorry to be leaving home. She seemed to think it was wrong of me to be glad.

"Don't you think, Auntie, it would be a shame for me to be sad when Papa and Mamma are giving me this costly trip that I may have treatment for my leg?" But Aunt Lovisa never would listen to reason. Her only reply was that she was the sort who could never leave home without regret, though of course it was only foolish of her.

Mother, obviously wishing to end the discussion between Auntie and me, arose, saying that it was time we were off. But before we left I wanted to go out to the kitchen to say good-bye to the maids; for I was to be away until spring.

As I passed through the bedroom on my way to the kitchen, Nurse Maja stopped me and asked if she might have a word with me. She looked so mysterious and solemn that I became quite alarmed. I stopped, of course, to hear what she had to tell me.

It seems that last summer she overheard Fru Wallroth ask Fru Afzelius whether it was true that Selma was to come to them next winter and take treatments at the Institute.

"Yes," Fru Afzelius had answered, "it is true." And then she had added that it was not surprising her parents wished to send Selma to Stockholm, but both she and her husband would rather have had one of the other girls, for Selma was so dull and unresponsive.

When Nurse Maja told me that, my heart was crushed. I stood stock-still, not knowing what to answer.

"You mustn't be angry with me, Selma, for telling you this," Nurse Maja said. "I meant it for your good. I only wanted to warn you so you wouldn't sit and mope, as you do sometimes, but be chatty and gay when you get to Stockholm. I think you are the nicest of all the Marbacka children, and I want everyone else to think so, too. That was why I had to tell you."

While she was talking I tried to think of a crushing retort.... At last I hit upon something telling, and to the point!

"Don't you remember that it says in the catechism,

"If you hear any evil of another, do not repeat it,
for silence hurts no one. You shall tell it neither
to friend nor to foe; and reveal it not if you can
consciously avoid it."

With that, I walked away, feeling that I had given Nurse Maja the rebuke she deserved for her talebearing. My distress was less acute now, but I was not nearly so sure of myself as I had been a moment earlier. When I said good-bye to Aunt Lovisa I kissed her hand. I think she understood that I wished to beg her pardon for admonishing her.

And when Mother wrapped her big fur coat around me to keep me nice and warm on the long drive to Kil, I nearly burst out crying. I felt so sorry to be leaving her and all those who loved me, to go to others who would rather not have me!

When I got up into the sleigh my heart ached dreadfully. I feared it would ache like that all the while I was in Stockholm. How should I ever be able to endure it until Spring!

Daniel is studying medicine at Upsala; so perhaps he could help me. When I asked him what one did for anyone who suffered pain in the heart, he only laughed and said that he would answer my question some other time; he was too sleepy now.

At Kil we bought third-class tickets, and when the

train arrived we were ushered into an empty compartment in which the odours of gin, foot sweat and I know not what else assailed our nostrils. We tried to air the place, but it grew so cold that we had to close the window again. I told Daniel that when I was rich I'd never travel third class.

Daniel gave me a look that took me in from head to foot and said in a casual tone, "Then I think you will have to travel third class as long as you live."

I couldn't help thinking of the passage in the Bible where it says, *"Mene, mene, tekel, upharsin,"* for today I have been measured and weighed and counted--and found wanting.

When the train began to move, Daniel took out a German anatomy and settled himself in a corner to study, while I took out my diary and began to write.

And now I have written five whole pages. It really is quite necessary to keep a diary. Looking up, I see that we have come all the way to Laxå station. The time has passed quickly despite the pain in my heart and my sadness--thanks to Elin Laurell!

Between Södertälje and Stockholm

Now I'll have to hurry, for I want to write a few lines to say that I am no longer sad, and my heart has stopped aching, and that is a blessed relief.

I know that we're nearing Stockholm, but I could not write before because the student sat with us until we came to Södertälje, when he said he must go back to his compartment to gather up his things before we arrived.

There were many old women down by the station who

offered small cakes for sale in little bags. I got two bags, one from the student and one from Daniel. It was very nice of them, although I have to admit that those cakes were pretty stale.

But now I must hasten to write about what took place after the student came into our compartment. First he talked with Daniel, of course; then after a little Daniel told him that I was his sister and my name was Selma and that I was going to Stockholm to stay until spring.

"How delightful for Selma!" said the student. Then he told us that his parents were Stockholmers but they resided now in Christiania. They loved Sweden more than any other country and wished their son to be brought up a Swede, and so he had grown up in the home of relatives in Stockholm. To his mind Stockholm was the best place in the whole world. The last two winters he had been at the University of Upsala and had spent the Christmas holidays in Christiania. But for life and gaiety it couldn't be compared to Stockholm.

"But you'll see for yourself, Selma, how it is," he said.

I answered, of course, that I had lived in Stockholm a whole winter and knew the city well.

"Five years ago!" said the astonished student. "But you were only a child then, so you couldn't have seen very much of it."

"I did, though," I replied. "I saw the whole city."

The student really must have loved Stockholm, for he asked me whether I had seen this or that or that, and there was not much that I was not familiar with. He said I must have a good memory, and thought it remarkable that

I had seen so many interesting things although I was but nine years old at the time.

The student and I became the best of friends, and before long he spoke only to me. For Daniel had merely passed through Stockholm on his way to Upsala; so he did not know the city as well as I did.

If Anna or Hilda Wallroth or Emma Laurell had been sitting here, opposite the student, they would surely have fallen in love with him, for he is so good-looking!

He has dark hair that curls over his forehead and one unruly lock that keeps falling down when he grows enthusiastic. He has large eyes that are so dark that I can't tell what colour they are, but they scintillate like black jewels. And he is also friendly and sympathetic. I wonder if he saw that I was sad when he came in and if that was why he spoke to me?

Naturally Daniel thought that what I said was not worth listening to, so he took up his book and began to read again. But I noticed that he was not very intent upon his reading, for all of a sudden he chuckled at something that was said.

Nurse Maja flashed across my mind as we were at the most interesting part of our conversation. It would have been well if she had sat in a corner of the compartment and heard how easily I talked with the student.

I thought, too, that when I came to Stockholm it would be a slight matter for me to show Aunt and Uncle that I was neither dull nor unresponsive. All I would have to do would be to sit down and talk to them as easily and frankly as I now talked with the student. Indeed, he did not find me dull; nor did Daniel, who sat chuckling behind his book.

The student and I discussed many topics besides Stockholm before we reached Södertälje. It was so easy to talk
to him; we were of one mind on many subjects, and I was
not afraid to say quite freely what I thought.

When he went his way at Södertälje the compartment
became singularly empty. But I was not at all depressed
as I had been earlier in the day. I felt a bit giddy, as I
feel even at this moment. Daniel rises and says, "Now
we are in Stockholm!" Auntie and Uncle are on the plat-
form awaiting us.

THE FIRST WEEK

January 21, 1873   *Written by Ulla's small lamp.*

I wonder if those who keep a diary ever record their
dreams? For I would like to write about a strange dream
I had last night that I cannot put out of my mind.

In the first place, I don't understand why I should have
dreamed about Marit of Sotbråten. I remember, of course,
that when Gerda was a small child, Nurse Maja used to
tell her about a poor girl who was called Marit of Sotbråten. She lived at Högbergssäter, where Maja came from,
and she was as mean and foolish as Maja was wise and
kind. She always ran about unwashed and snotty, her tan-
gled hair hanging over her eyes. One couldn't imagine a
girl like Marit of Sotbråten ever combing her hair, and as
for her clothes--they were nothing but rags. She seemed
more akin to the trolls of Storsnipan than to human beings,
Nurse Maja declared; and she was never known to do anything but raise mischief.

And if some morning Gerda wouldn't be washed or have

her hair combed, then Marit of Sotbråten, seated on the highest peak of Storsnipan, laughed and shrieked for joy, as her greatest delight was to see unwashed and uncombed children of the gentry. And if Gerda would not go to sleep of an evening but wanted to hear more stories, then Marit of Sotbråten came riding across the hills to crawl into bed with her. As she rode down Käglabacken, the stones rolling before and behind, striking sparks and rumbling like a thunderstorm, there was nothing for Gerda to do but to draw the covers over her ears and go to sleep in a jiffy, to escape the horrid bedfellow.

Nurse Maja, however, never attempted to frighten me with Marit of Sotbråten, for I was too old and wise to believe such ridiculous tales. For that reason it seems strange that Marit should have followed me here to Stockholm.

Just the same I dreamed last night that I lay on the pretty white sofa in the nursery, when I saw, sitting above me on the arm of the sofa, a filthy, repulsive girl. She tossed her head so that the tufts of matted hair flew in every direction, and sat swinging her legs. I knew at once that she was Marit of Sotbråten. I was both frightened and angry and ordered her to go back to Högbergssäter at once. Then she crept in under the bedcovers, where she quickly became as small and narrow as an earthworm. Before I knew what she meant to do she had crawled into my ear. It was such a horrible sensation having a long worm crawling around in my head that I gave a shriek--and with that, I awoke.

I know now that I had only been dreaming and that Marit of Sotbråten has not followed me to Stockholm. And

yet, I could not shake off the sensation that a worm was
crawling around in my head. And while I lay there half
awake and tormented by my fear of the worm, I felt almost
certain that Nurse Maja had sent Marit upon me because I
had rebuked her for talebearing, quoting Scripture as my
authority.

Nurse Maja was born at Högbergssäter, where there
are a lot of witches who can send sickness and other ills
upon those they have an evil eye for. Of course I wouldn't
say positively that the witches had taught their tricks to
Maja, but I was not so far from believing they had. She
was angry with me for ignoring her good intentions, and
wanted to be avenged. And now I was no longer Selma
Lagerlöf, but had turned into a wicked and foolish little
imp whose name was Marit of Sotbråten.

It all seemed so real and true that I was frightened
to the point of despair, and I cried a long while over my
plight before I fell asleep again. Next morning I was my
old self, and then I laughed at myself for having imagined
anything so absurd. But I wondered if, after all, there
was not some truth in that dream.

Saturday, January 25   *In the parlour at Uncle Oriel's.*

I have found that it is no pleasure to keep a diary unless one writes the truth. I had plenty of time to write
last evening, but something happened that I was ashamed
to set down. I can't understand myself. I seem to have
become so wild and unruly that I've lost all control of myself, which is something I have rarely done before.

Every evening, after my cousins have gone to bed,
Auntie and I go into the parlour, she to knit at a shawl

and I to crochet insertion. Sometimes Uncle comes in to smoke his long pipe while he reads the daily news. One evening when he came into the parlour he carried a small, thick book. I wondered what sort of book it could be that was so interesting as to make Uncle forget his newspaper, when he suddenly looked up at me and said:

"This book you are not to read. Remember that!"

I promised to remember, and no more was said about the matter. But yesterday morning as I sat down at the piano to run through my lesson, Uncle and Auntie came in. Uncle was so busy talking to Auntie that he paid no attention to me as I struggled with Czerny's études. He was telling Auntie about a Frenchman who had attempted to murder Ludwig XIII and had been broken upon the wheel in the presence of the Court and all the servitors.

As I sat playing I could catch only fragments of what was being said, but I had a burning desire to find out how all this had come to pass. The worst of it was, I suspected that Uncle had read it all in the book that I was forbidden to touch.

I wouldn't have touched it, either, had I been my real self. Although I have many faults, I generally keep my word.

At noon, when I return from the Institute, I have to rest for an hour. I usually lie down on the sofa in the bedroom, but yesterday that room was being cleaned; so Auntie said I could lie on the lounge in Uncle's room, as he had gone out. As I stretched myself out on the couch I saw on the table, within arm's reach, the thick little book. I picked it up and opened it to see what kind of book it was.

When I found it was only a French history, I thought it very childish of Uncle to forbid me to read it, for history is something everyone who wishes may read. I began to turn the leaves, and just as I had found the place about the torture, I heard footsteps in the hall; but I am so obtuse nowadays that it didn't occur to me that it might be Uncle. The next moment he was standing in the doorway while I lay reading the forbidden book! I never felt so embarrassed in my life.

I sprang up and quickly replaced the book on the table; then I begged Uncle's pardon for being so curious to see what sort of book it was that I should not read. Uncle, however, was not so very angry at me.

"I can understand," he said, "that you are the sort who cannot breathe unless you have your nose buried in a book. Hereafter I shall leave the key to my bookcase in the lock so that you may read Sir Walter Scott as much as you like, but you must let the other books alone."

It was very kind of Uncle, and I thanked him as graciously as I could. But just the same I feel terribly ashamed. I blush if he only looks at me. I'm afraid he must think me always disobedient, and that no one can rely on any of my promises. He does not know that I am changed and that I am no longer my real self.

THE FOURTH WEEK

Monday, February 10

In the churchyard there are smooth and even gravel paths where walking is easy. But I'm anxious to get past it as quickly as possible so as not to encounter the schoolboys. Klara School lies at the corner of the churchyard;

at recess the boys rush out to the large grave mounds and stone caskets near the church, where they play at war, and I fear that they will knock me down.

I feel a little afraid of those schoolboys, but at the same time it is pleasant to know that they still hold forth in Klara Churchyard just as in August Blanche's time. They look like regular ruffians; but no matter, for I know from August Blanche's stories that they are high-minded and chivalrous and that many of them will be generals and bishops and will marry beautiful daughters of the nobility.

There is one boy in particular. He is poorly clad like the others, but he is not quite so wild. I have often noticed that he stands looking on while his comrades are fighting their hardest. He has beautiful blue eyes and perhaps, when he is full-grown... Anyhow, he is the only one who could have been the boy to receive "a waistcoat with pearl buttons as a birthday present from his mamma," as the storybook says.

One day I saw the quiet boy sitting with head bowed, all alone on the largest of the stone coffins. To me it was as though Victor Ekström sat there and wept over his mother's death. I stopped in front of him, as I wished to say something comforting--for I felt so well acquainted with that boy! I was waiting until I could think of something really nice to say, when he suddenly raised his head, pulled a wry face and, with a savage look, roared at me:

"Why do you stand there glaring at me, you limping devil's spawn!"

I made no retort, but went on my way. But I wished that the elegant couple who lay in the big stone coffin would raise the lid a trifle and tweak his nose.

When that boy called me a limping devil's spawn I thought of my student. He has only seen me sitting in the railway compartment and standing by the window; he has never seen me walk. So he does not know that I am lame. I wonder how it will be when he finds out.

THE FIFTH WEEK

The evening of Thursday, February 20. *In the bedroom.*

I have had such long and difficult English lessons this week that I could find no time to open my diary. But I must write, because I've met a young girl who may serve as a model on which to pattern my life, so that I, too, may become a pleasant companion.

This morning I had little to do, so I sat with Auntie in her bedroom and crocheted while I listened to her stories about Stockholmers. But just as we were having the coziest time, a gentleman called. It was Squire W. of Västerås--an old friend of Uncle Oriel's who has come to Stockholm to attend a business conference. He has brought his daughter with him, and asked if she might dine with the Afzelius family today.

Auntie laughingly assured him that Fröken W. was very welcome to have dinner with them, and added that if she felt lonely she could come whenever she wished. But the Squire thought that while Signe (that is her name) was in Stockholm she would want to visit as many shops as possible. So it was agreed that she need not come before half-past three, which is our regular dinner hour.

When this had been settled Herr W. left. Auntie told me that it would not be an easy matter to entertain young

Fröken W., for she had heard that the girl was terribly spoiled. Well, at least she would have Cook put another cake in the oven for dessert and lay a fresh cloth on the table. Auntie also advised me to change my collar and cuffs, because the W.s of Västerås are said to be very elegant and refined folk.

Fröken W. did not arrive on the stroke of half-past three, the time set. Nor did she come at three thirty-five; nor yet at three-forty did she appear. We wondered if she had forgotten the house number or had been run over by a brewery wagon since she, who was from the country, naturally was not used to the heavy traffic on the streets of Stockholm.

Uncle had flung himself into the large armchair in the bedroom, saying that he would take his after-dinner nap before the meal. Auntie went time and again out to the kitchen to see whether the cake had fallen or if it still held up. It was most inconsiderate of Fröken W. to be so late. But what a dreadful calamity it would be if something had befallen the girl who is the apple of her father's eye.

At that moment there was a ring at the doorbell, and I thought how embarrassed I would be if I were a quarter of an hour late, and I felt very sorry for Fröken W.

When she came into the parlour, where we were waiting for her, she did not appear to be at all sorry. She rushed up to Auntie and Uncle, gave each a hug, kissed them on both cheeks, and asked if she might call them Aunt and Uncle. Then she kissed Elin and Allan and me right on the mouth and said we should call her Signe. She was so gay and friendly that we were all charmed with her the moment she appeared.

I need not have been the least bit anxious on her ac-
count. Fröken W. expressed no regret for being late and
offered no apology. It sounded rather as though she wished
to be commended for coming as early as she did. There
were such wonderful shops here in Stockholm! Think of
Leya's (perhaps it was best not to think of the shops!),
but think of Magnusson's on Västerlånggata. Fröken W.
(perhaps I ought to say Signe, since she has waived all
titles between her and me) ran out into the hall and came
back with all her parcels to show us what she had bought.
Although Uncle Oriel had said a little while before that he
was hungry enough to devour the girl herself, and although
Auntie had been so uneasy about the cake, they now gave
themselves time to look at one purchase after another.
When Fröken W. (there, I've written "Fröken W." again!
Perhaps it will be best to keep on the way I have begun.)
When Fröken W. unrolled a dress pattern of blue linen,
she gave a cry of delight. Then, directly afterward, she
raised her eyebrows clear up to her hairline, and said in
a voice full of anxiety that she knew the other Västerås
girls would die of envy when they saw this dress pattern.
She was afraid they would throw themselves into Lake
Mäleren the instant they beheld it.

I did not think Fröken W. was pretty, but nevertheless
it was impossible not to keep looking at her. When Fröken W. was not talking, which was rarely, she looked like
the average young girl. Mamma used to say that certain
persons have a striking appearance, but that couldn't be
said of Fröken W. She has light, curly hair, a sweet little
mouth, white teeth, pink-and-white complexion, blue eyes

as round as a ball, and a pug nose. I have seen many girls who resemble her, yet in some way she is different-ly constituted from the girls I have met. She was not at all embarrassed by her pug nose, but seemed to like to show it and to show the round baby eyes and the funny little tufts of hair that passed for eyebrows.

I gazed at Fröken W. as much as I dared without seeming to be rude, for I could learn so much from her. It was strange that she did not speak of the things one usually talks about here in Stockholm--except the shops, of course. She did not mention the royal family, the the-atre or the Academy of Art. She talked only of Västerås.

Uncle Oriel is over fifty years old, and Aunt Georgina is at least forty, yet she talked to them as though they were but seventeen. The strange thing about it was that this seemed the proper way to approach them.

She told of a sleighing party which had afforded her much amusement--recounting for Uncle and Auntie all the stupid nonsense the gentleman had said to her while dri-ving. Just as his love-making grew most intense she jerked a rein so that the horse went down in the ditch and the sleigh overturned. One must have some excitement, she said, when out on a sleighing party.

When she said that, she turned her round baby eyes toward heaven, and the retroussé nose went up in the air as much as to say she had only given him his just deserts. But her eyebrows went up in astonishment that she could have been so naughty.

Friday morning, February 21.   *In the sitting room.*
I have thought all day of Fröken W. Now I know what

Aunt Georgina meant when she said that I was dull and unresponsive. I understand that she wishes me to be like
Fröken W.--friendly and talkative and amusing and open
and natural as every young girl ought to be.

But how, how, oh how, am I to become like her!

Much as I admired Fröken W., I felt rather down-
hearted after she had gone because I was so unlike her.
Auntie and Uncle had gone to the theatre, invited by Squire
W., and I sat in the bedchamber writing until I grew sleepy
and went to bed.

I had not slept long when I awoke. Auntie had come
home from the theatre and stopped in the nursery to talk
with Ulla, who had been sitting up for her. I heard them
speak of a young girl whom they praised extravagantly. I
understood, of course, they were speaking of Fröken W.
That made me keep my eyes shut and pretend to be asleep.
I admired Fröken W. greatly and wanted so much to be
like her, but in any case...

"Ulla, don't you think she is a very nice and well-
brought-up young girl?" said Auntie.

"Do you know, Fru," answered Ulla, in her clear and
positive voice, "I don't believe you could find a nicer or
a better-behaved young girl anywhere."

"No airs, nor stories about young men. She comes
and goes as she should. And she is gifted, too, Ulla.
Baroness H. says she speaks English remarkably well.

I was not a little astonished that the Baroness H.
knew all about Fröken W. It was also queer that Auntie
should say she had no stories to tell about gentlemen.

"The little girl who was here today was very sweet,"
Auntie continued. "But, Ulla, don't you think it would be

rather trying to have a person like her living in your home?"

"Yes, it would be rather trying at times," Ulla conceded.

I understood now that it was of me they were speaking, and I was so happy that I wanted to jump out of bed and give Auntie a great big hug. But then I thought that perhaps she might be angry if she knew that I had been listening--and I kept still.

THE SIXTH WEEK

Monday, 24 February. *In the parlour.*

Cousin Allan has a toy that I never tire of looking at. It is a small, inexpensive toy; in fact, it is only a stick of wood about the length of my hand. But the remarkable thing about it is that it can fly.

At one end of the stick is a small wheel with eight tiny wings made of stiff paper. At the other end is a little "winch" of steel wire, and between the wheel and the winch runs an elastic band.

When Allan wants the stick to fly he turns the winch round and round until the rubber band is stretched to its utmost. He twists the winch until it can't turn, and puts the toy down. The rubber band begins to lose its tautness, thereby setting the paper wheel in motion. It turns very fast and, after two or three revolutions, it shoots upward, drawing the stick along. If the band has been drawn tight enough, the stick goes up all the way to the ceiling, flying back and forth up there, knocking against the plaster, as if it would bore its way out to the open.

The stick is green, and the wings on the wheel are red and white. When the little machine flies round the room, it looks exactly as if it were a witch flying on a broomstick.

Yesterday afternoon, as I sat studying my lesson, Allan wound up his toy and let it fly. I shut my grammar and followed it with my eyes. As the toy rose toward the ceiling it flashed upon me that one ought to be able to make a real flying machine--one that could be used by man, with the little flying stick as a pattern.

At first I thought that this was just nonsense; but now I'm beginning to wonder if it wouldn't be a good idea. It would be a great pleasure for us human beings to be able to travel by air. But I don't believe the big gas-filled balloons have any future. They are forever bursting, and even if they do not burst they move with the wind and are carried hither and thither, no one knows where.

But if one had a large enough wheel with steady wings and a connecting rod, like the wheel on a spindle, at which one could sit and work with the feet to make the wheel revolve, I think that would be a good flying machine.

Tuesday, February 25.

I lay thinking of the flying machine all the morning. Since such big birds as cranes and geese can fly, it ought to be possible for men to fly also. But it all depends, of course, upon whether one can make the wheel turn fast enough.

Wednesday, February 26.

I have stopped thinking of the student, and I don't try

to write stories. It is far more important that I figure out how my flying machine should be constructed. Of course I know it can't be finished before I am grown, but there's no harm in having everything well thought out.

Thursday, February 27.

When my machine is ready I'm going to fly to Stockholm. How the Stockholmers will stare and how they will wonder what kind of bird that is! Centralplan will be black with people gazing, spellbound, at the sky. And when Aunt Georgina, sitting at the bedroom window sewing, sees all the people, she calls to Uncle Oriel and Ulla to come and look out.

And when the airship comes near, it flies back and forth a couple of times over Centralplan that the people may behold it; then, to the amazement of everyone, it descends in the yard of Klara Strandgata Number 7.

I wonder what Uncle Oriel will say then.

But I shall tell him, at once, that it was here at Number 7, with Aunt and Uncle, that I caught the idea for the great invention, and because of that I have made my first journey by air to their home.

THE TENTH WEEK

Tuesday, March 25, Annunciation Day

(The cook at Selma's Aunt's house is fond of touring through a museum of medical exhibits in Stockholm. Ordinarily, the collection is closed to children, but the cook happens to know the wife of the museum's watchman, who, somewhat reluctantly, takes Selma and her cousins into the forbidden chambers of the Carolinian Institute.)

We came to a room where the shelves and tables were covered with big glass jars.

"Look over here, Selma," said the watchman's wife. "Can you guess what this is?... Well, it is a child with two heads."

"And the hideous thing that lies in this jar has been dug from the belly of a human being," the young niece told us.

Next they showed us plaster casts of clubfeet, and hands with articular nodes.

"I wish I were a man," said the cook, "so that I could be a doctor and go here day in and day out."

The last thing we saw was a closet in the attic where a row of skeletons had been set up. One of them was so huge that we had to ask whether it was the skeleton of a human being.

"Yes indeed," said the watchman's wife. "It is the skeleton of a woman known as 'Long Lapska.' She was the most discussed freak of nature in her time."

When we came down from the attic I was all tired out and did not want to see any more exhibits. But the cook said that the one we were coming to was the most interesting of all.

"It is down in the basement," she said. Turning to her aunt, she spoke in a lowered voice. "Have any come in today?"

"Yes," said her aunt; "but not many--only four. But are you going down there alone? That's not for children to see, you know."

The cook said that since we had seen everything else,

we should also be allowed to see this; for this was something we could never forget. And so the kind wife of the watchman gave way.

She conducted us down the basement stairs, but here such a horrible stench assailed our nostrils that we stopped short.

"They are lying under water," said the watchman's wife; "but all the same, it's impossible to keep them fresh. There's no smell so penetrating as the odour of a cadaver."

We children were then told that all who had made away with themselves were brought here for the students who were learning to be doctors to dissect.

We stepped into a large cellar room which was well lighted, but where the stench was so overpowering that we had to hold our hands to our noses.

"I wonder if we hadn't better turn back," said the watchman's wife.

"Only for a moment," the cook said, as she opened a door.

I stood close beside her and looked into a dim oblong room. Along one side of the wall there was a wide bunk, and above it trickled a steady stream of water. On the bunk lay four bodies, their heads resting against the wall, their feet down in the bunk, as in a big double bed.

I saw them only for a second, but I remember exactly how they looked. The one nearest the door was an old man with a black beard streaked with gray and a long pointed nose. He wore a coat that reached down to his feet, but they were bare and full of knots and sores. But for the feet, the old man would not have been hard to look at.

Beside the old man lay a young woman (she was not so very young, though; I should say her age was about thirty). She was tall and dreadfully bloated; her clothes were worn threadbare in several places so that the dead-white skin showed through. The face was not so bloated as the body, and I could see that she had been beautiful.

At her side lay a boy of about five or six years. His cap was drawn down over his face, but one side of his body was bare, and through a large wound the entrails oozed out.

The fourth was only a bundle of black clothing. I think there was a man inside, but one couldn't be certain of that. A foot stuck out here, there a hand. The hair showed where the feet should have been, and the chin was thrust forward from under the elbow. He must have been ground to pieces and gathered up.

That much I saw before the watchman's wife came forward and shut the door.

As we went up the stairs our cook said that today the dead were a rather ghastly sight, to which the watchman's wife replied rather brusquely that they were about as usual. She evidently did not approve of their having been shown to us children.

Though I had seen all the dead plainly, I had been moved most deeply by the woman who had drowned herself. To think that she had been so unhappy that she had thrown herself into the lake!

I had heard of such things and read about them many times, but I had never before understood what they meant. No, I had not understood a single one of all the stories of unhappiness I had read about in books.

It was so terrible that this was real!

I thought of those who lay sick, and of cripples; but first and last of those who were so unhappy that they did not want to live.

Could I ever be happy again now that I knew there was so much evil in the world? Never again, in all my life, would I be able to laugh or play or go to the theatre. Never again would I be the same as when I left home in the morning. Then, when we crossed the Kungsholm Bridge, I thought the view was beautiful. But I saw no beauty on my way back. Surely I could never again think anything in this world lovely.

As I walked home I thought that Stockholm was an ugly city; that the water under me was full of frogs and big, slimy lizards. I thought that all whom I met on the bridge were rotting corpses.

March 26--the day after Annunciation Day.

I wrote last Monday that I would have to record a remarkable experience I had while looking at Axel Oxenstierna. But perhaps I'd better take that back, for when I think straight about the matter I know that it was only an illusion. But the illusion was so beautiful, while it seemed real and true, that just the thought of it fills me with awe. But now that I know it wasn't real, why write about it in my daybook? Yet surely it will do no harm to relate it, if at the same time I say the incident was only something I imagined.

On Monday morning when I was in the parlour ready to write in my diary about the Carolinian Institute, I sat awhile looking at the lovely painting of Charles X Gustaf

at the deathbed of Axel Oxenstierna. It did my eyes good
to rest upon this picture after all the gruesome things they
had seen the previous day. But my joy was not for long.
The canvas soon disappeared, and in its place was the bunk
in the mortuary with the four bodies lying there so miser-
ably poor and forsaken, the spray playing upon them all
the while.

Sunday afternoon I saw them before me, and after I
had gone to bed that night, and when I awoke next morning. I felt terribly unhappy about them, so it was no wonder they were with me continually.

It would have been a comfort to me if I could have
helped them in some way. The thought of what they must
have suffered in life was so painful! If at least I could
have decorated their last resting place a little!

But how could I help? For all I could do they would
have to lie as they were. It was all so dreadful!

And then of a sudden I saw the beautiful painting with
all its rich draperies and carpets, and I said to myself,
"If one only had such lovely draperies to spread over them!"

It was a stupid thought. These were only painted draperies and could not be spread over anything. But all the
same I went up to the painting and begged Axel Oxenstierna
to let me have his beautiful bedcovers to spread over the
four bodies that they would not have to lie there so wretch-
edly exposed. You see, he was dead, too, and he could
do things, perhaps, that were impossible to us who are
living.

I knew all the while that this was only fancy. Yet it
wasn't altogether make-believe, either.

I told Axel Oxenstierna that I knew that in his lifetime

he had been as a father to the Swedish people, and I implored him now to take pity on the four poor unfortunates; for they, too, were Swedes, though of a later age than his.

While I was asking the help of Axel Oxenstierna, I saw as it were before me the mortuary and the bunk where the four bodies lay. It was only an illusion, of course, but all at once I seemed to see a lovely shimmer envelop them.

I turned my eyes once more upon Axel Oxenstierna. He lay there, quiet as always; but the beautiful light grew more and more distinct as it spread over the four dead bodies on the bunk.

I stood still, not daring to move. For it was--how shall I say?... Now, as I saw the mortuary before me, a wave of light lay over the four. They were entirely enveloped by the light, and I could see them no more.

I remembered them just as well as before, but I did not see them.

To be sure, I believe in the power of the dead, but I also know that Selma Ottilia Lovisa Lagerlöf is inclined to imagine things that are utterly impossible.

March 27, 1873.

Day before yesterday was Annunciation Day of the Virgin Mary, and Auntie asked me if I would like to go with her to the Catholic church. It was all the same to me whether I went here or there, and I immediately said, "Yes."

We went in time to get excellent seats far forward, where we could see the priests in their gorgeous robes and the small altar boys who ran back and forth inside

the altar railing, moving books, genuflecting, and swinging
censers.

My heart ached for the poor girl who had been so unhappy that she went and drowned herself, and I did not
follow the service. I did not even notice when the choir
began to sing, for I sat grieving over her death as though
I had known and loved her.

As I was lamenting my loss I heard a high, clear
voice reverberating throughout the church. I was astonished, for I had never heard such heavenly music. I had
attended the Catholic church before with Auntie, and on
coming out she had always praised the beautiful singing.
But I myself could not say that it was beautiful. I wondered at times if there was not something wrong with my
ears, that I could not understand what others found so en-
chanting.

But now, as I sat there grieving over the dead, I
heard every tone distinctly, and marvelled at the beauty
of it all. I thought that it was a greeting from the poor
suicide. It was she who had caused my ears to be opened
that I might hear the song on just that day.

And I thought, also, that she told me through the song
that I should not mourn for her any longer. She heard
singing far more glorious than that to which I listened, and
she remembered no more the sufferings of her earthly life.

Auntie saw that I was weeping. She bent down and
asked me if I felt ill. I shook my head and tried to whis-
per that I was crying because the song was so beautiful.

"It is indeed," Auntie whispered back. "I feel like
weeping with you."

After that we sat holding hands, Auntie and I, as long
as the song lasted.

Marie Bashkirtseff

Marie Bashkirtseff was a very wealthy Russian girl who lived with her mother in France and Italy from the time her parents separated when she was ten.

This excerpt begins when she was fourteen and goes through her eighteenth year. She is beset by all the perplexing problems of youth: what to become when she grows up, how to find someone to love her, and an all-consuming need for attention and recognition.

Bored, restless, disliking her family and most everyone she knew, Marie really only found herself when at eighteen she began serious work as an artist.

Though certainly not the most "heartful" of the girls (one early reviewer of the diary called her "a horrid little pig"), her perception about herself and her world is so acute and her honesty so captivating that we can not help but be drawn to her despite her excesses of vanity and ambition and her overwhelming contempt for others.

Her continual fears of dying young and leaving little behind to show for her life were actualized when she died at twenty-four of tuberculosis. However, she is widely known for this diary, which is as she had planned it.

1860 - 1884

Marie Bashkirtseff

Tuesday, July 6.

Read this, good people, and profit by it! This journal is the most useful and the most instructive of all the books that were or ever will be written. It is the transcript of a woman's life--her thoughts and hopes, her deceptions, meannesses, good qualities, sorrows and joys. I am not yet altogether a woman, but I shall be. One may follow me here from childhood to death. For the life of any one -- one's entire life, without concealment or disguise--is always a grand and interesting spectacle.

Friday, July 16.

In regard to the transference of love, all I possess at present is concentrated on Victor, one of my dogs. I breakfast with him sitting opposite to me, his fine, large head resting on the table. Let us love dogs; let us love only dogs! Men and cats are unworthy creatures. And yet a dog is a filthy animal. He looks at you with hungry eyes while you eat; he follows you about for the sake of his dinner. Yet I never feed my dogs and they love me. And men--do not they ask to be fed? Are they not voracious and mercenary?...

My hair, fastened in a Psyche knot, is redder than ever. In a woolen gown of a peculiar white, well-fitting and graceful, and a lace handkerchief around my neck, I look like one of the portraits of the First Empire; in order to make the picture complete I should be seated under a tree, holding a book in my hand. I love to be alone before a looking-glass, and to admire my hands, so fine and white, and faintly rosy in the palms.

Perhaps it is stupid to praise one's-self in this way, but people who write always describe their heroine, and I am my heroine. And it would be ridiculous for me to lower or belittle myself through false modesty. One makes little of one's-self in conversation, because one is sure of being contradicted, but if I were to do so in writing, every one would believe I was speaking the truth, and that I was ugly and stupid, and that would be absurd!

Fortunately or unfortunately, I esteem myself so great a treasure that I think there is no one worthy of me, and those who raise their eyes to this treasure are regarded by me as hardly worthy of pity. I think myself a divinity, and I cannot conceive how a man like G.--- should fancy he could please me. I could scarcely treat a king as an equal. I think that is as it should be. I look down on men from such a height that they find me charming, for it is not becoming to despise those who are so far beneath us. I regard them as a hare would regard a mouse.

Nice, Italy. Friday, October 1, 1875.

I despise men profoundly and from conviction. I expect nothing good from them. I should be satisfied after all my waiting to find one good and perfect soul. Those who are good are stupid, and those who are intelligent are either too false or too self-conceited to be good. Besides, every human being is by nature selfish, and find goodness for me if you can in an egotist. Self-interest, deceit, intrigue, envy, these are what you will find. Happy are they who possess ambition -- that is a noble passion, through vanity or through ambition one seeks to appear well in the eyes of others sometimes, and that is better than not at all. Well, my child, have you come to the end of your philosophy? For the moment, yes. In this way, at least, I shall suffer fewer disappointments. No meanness will grieve me, no base action surprise me. The day will doubtless come when I shall think I have found a man, but, if so, I shall deceive myself wofully. I can very well foresee that day; I shall then be blind. I say this now while I can see clearly. But in that case why live; since there is nothing but meanness and wickedness in the world? Why? Because I am reconciled to the knowledge that this is so; because, whatever people may say, life is very beautiful. And because, if one does not analyze too deeply, one may live happily. To count neither on friendship nor gratitude, nor loyalty nor honesty; to elevate one's-self courageously above the meannesses of humanity, and take one's stand between them and God; to get all one can out of life, and that quickly; to do no injury to one's fellow-beings; to make

one's life luxurious and magnificent; to be independent, so
far as it be possible, of others; to possess power!--yes,
power!--no matter by what means!--this is to be feared
and respected; this is to be strong, and that is the height
of human felicity, because one's fellow-beings are then
muzzled, and either through cowardice or for other reasons
will not seek to tear one to pieces.

Is it not strange to hear me reason in this way? Yes,
but this manner of reasoning in a young creature like me
is but another proof of how bad the world is; it must be
thoroughly saturated with wickedness to have so saddened
me in so short a time. I am only fifteen....

Why can one never speak without exaggeration?...
There are peaceful souls, there are beautiful actions and
honest hearts, but they are so rarely to be met with that
one must not confound them with the rest of the world.

Friday, March 31.

My God, do not punish me for my vanity. I swear to
you that I am good at heart, incapable of cowardice or
baseness. I am ambitious--that is my greatest fault! The
beauties and the ruins of Rome made me dizzy. I should
like to be Caesar, Augustus, Marcus Aurelius, Nero, Cara-
calla, Satan, the Pope! I should like to be all these--and
I am nothing.

Wednesday, April 5.

I paint and I read, but that is not enough. For a vain
creature like me it is best to devote one's-self entirely to
painting, because that is imperishable.

I shall be neither a poet nor a philosopher, nor a *sa-*

vante. I can be nothing more than a singer and a painter. But that is always something. And then I want to be talked of by everybody, which is the principal thing. Stern moralists, do not shrug your shoulders and censure me with an affected indifference for worldly things because I speak in this way. If you were more just you would confess that you yourselves are the same at heart! You take very good care not to let it be seen, but that does not prevent you from knowing in your inmost souls that I speak the truth.

Wednesday, May 31.

Ask those who know me best what they think of my disposition, and they will tell you that I am the gayest, the most self-reliant person they ever saw, for I experience a singular pleasure in appearing haughty and happy, invulnerable to a wound from any quarter, and I delight in taking part in discussions of all sorts, both serious and playful. Here you see me as I am. To the world I am altogether different. One would suppose, to see me, that I had never had a care in my life, and that I was accustomed to bend circumstances and people alike to my will.

Sunday, July 2.

Oh, what heat! Oh, what *ennui*! But I am wrong to say *ennui* (that one can never feel who has so many resources within one's-self as I have.) I do not feel *ennui*; for I read, I sing, I paint, I dream; but I am restless and sorrowful. Is my poor young life, then, doomed to be spent in eating and drinking, and domestic quarrels. Woman lives from sixteen to forty. I tremble at the thought of losing even a single month of my life. If this is to be,

why have I studied, and sought to know more than other
women, priding myself on being as learned as great men
are said in their biographies to have been.

If this is to be so, why have I studied and reflected?
Why were genius and beauty and the gift of song bestowed
upon me? That I might wither in obscurity and die of sad-
ness. If I had been ignorant and stupid I might then, perhaps, have been happy. Not a living soul with whom to
exchange a word! One's family does not suffice for a creature of sixteen--above all, a creature such as I am. Grand-
papa, it is true, is a man of intelligence, but he is old and
blind; he irritates one with his eternal complaints about the
dinner and about his servant Triphon.

Mamma has a good deal of intelligence, very little
learning, no knowledge of the world, no tact whatever, and
her faculties have deteriorated through thinking of nothing
but the servants, my health, and the dogs.

Nice, Wednesday, May 23.

Oh, when I think that we have only a single life to live,
and that every moment that passes brings us nearer death,
I am ready to go distracted!

I do not fear death, but life is so short that to waste
it is infamous.

I try to tranquilize my mind by thinking that I shall
certainly begin work in earnest this winter. But the thought
of my seventeen years makes me blush to the roots of my
hair. Almost seventeen, and what have I accomplished?
Nothing! This thought crushes me.

I think of all the famous men and women who acquired
their celebrity late in life, in order to console myself; but

seventeen years for a man are nothing, while for a woman they are equal to twenty-three for a man.

Wednesday, July 18.

I want to express myself quite naturally, and if I make use of a few figures of speech, do not think it is for embellishment; oh, no! it is simply for the purpose of describing as nearly as possible the confusion of my thoughts.

It vexes me greatly to be able to write nothing that is pathetic. I long so much to make others feel what I feel! I weep, and I say I *weep*! That is not what I want. I want to make you feel the whole thing-- I want to touch your hearts!

That will come, and other things will come with it, but it must not be sought after.

Tuesday, August 27.

I, eighteen years old--it is absurd! My talents still undeveloped, my hopes, my passions, my caprices, will be ridiculous at eighteen. To begin to learn to paint at eighteen, when one has had the pretension of being able to do everything quicker and better than other people!

There are people who deceive others, but I have deceived myself.

Thursday, September 6.

I have resolved to remain in Paris, where I will pursue my studies, going to a watering-place in the summer for relaxation. All my caprices are exhausted. And I feel that the moment has at last come to pause in my course. With my abilities, in two years I shall have made up for lost time.

So, then, in the name of the Father, of the Son, and of the Holy Ghost, and may the divine protection be with me. This is not a resolution made to be broken, like so many former ones, but a final one.

Paris, Tuesday, October 2.

Today we removed our belongings to 71 Champs Elysses. Notwithstanding the confusion I found time to go to the *atelier Julian*, the only one of any note here for women.

The day passes quickly when one draws from eight in the morning till noon, and from one in the afternoon to five. Only to go to the studio and back takes almost an hour and a half. To-day I arrived a little late, so that I worked but six hours.

When I think of the entire years that I have lost it makes me angry enough to give up everything! But that would only make matters worse. Come, be miserable and hateful as you will, but be satisfied, at least, to have at last succeeded in making a beginning. And I might have begun at thirteen? Four entire years lost!

At last I am working with artists--real artists, who have exhibited in the *Salon*, and whose pictures are bought-- who even give lessons themselves.

Julian is satisfied with the beginning I have made. "By the end of the winter," he said to me, "you will be able to paint very good portraits."

He says some of the women pupils give as much promise as the men; I would have worked with the latter but that they smoke, and then there is no difference in the work.

Formerly the women pupils did not draw from the nude, but since they have been admitted to the Academy there is no difference made in that respect between them and the men.

The servant at the studio is just like one of those described in novels.

"I have always lived among artists," she says, "and I am not by any means one of the *bourgeoisie*; I am an artist."

I am happy, happy!

Friday, October 5.

"Did you do that by yourself?" M. Julian asked me on entering the studio to-day.

"Yes, Monsieur."

I grew as red as if I had told a falsehood.

"Well, I am satisfied with it, very well satisfied with it."

"Very well satisfied."

In the studio all distinctions disappear. One has neither name nor family; one is no longer the daughter of one's mother, one is one's-self,--an individual,--and one has before one art, and nothing else. One feels so happy, so free, so proud!

At last I am what I have so long wished to be. I have wished for it so long that I scarcely believe it now to be true.

Friday, January 4, 1878.

How strange it is that my old nature should lie so completely dormant. Scarce a trace of it is to be seen.

Occasionally some souvenir of the past reawakens the old bitterness, but I immediately turn my thoughts to--to what? To art.

Is this, then, the final transformation? I have so long and so eagerly pursued this aim, this means of contriving to live without passing the day cursing myself or the rest of creation, that I can scarcely believe that I have found it.

I begin to become what I desired to be, confident in my own powers, outwardly tranquil. I avoid quarrels and intrigues; I am scarcely ever without some useful occupation.

Monday, April 29.

There is no better way of spending the time from six in the morning till eight in the evening, taking out an hour and a half for breakfast, than in some regular occupation.

Changing the subject: I will tell you that I think I shall never be seriously in love. I invariably discover something to laugh at in the man, and that is the end of it. If he is not ridiculous, he is stupid, or awkward, or tiresome; in fine, there is always something, if it were only the tip of his ear.

Thanks to my readiness in discovering the defects of people, not all the Adonises in the world could tempt me to fall in love.

Nelly Ptaschkina

Nelly Ptaschkina kept a diary during the tumultuous time of the Russian Revolution. In it she recorded some of the events of the day, but mostly she used her diary to explore her own feelings. She wrote almost nightly from the time she was ten. Parts of the diary were lost as she and her family fled the Bolsheviks, but several copy books which covered her fourteenth and fifteenth years were saved by her mother and published in Nelly's memory.

In 1918, when Nelly was fifteen, she wrote of having a presentiment of her death. She pictured herself falling over a precipice, "plunging headlong into the chasm." July 2, 1920, she fell from an enormous height on Mont Blanc into a rushing torrent. Later her body washed ashore downstream and she was buried in Paris.

1903 - 1920

Nelly Ptaschkina

January 15, 1918

It has come into my mind that I have a kind of dual nature. It is pleasant, for I have a little of everything, but it is also annoying because I cannot define what I really am. I think it is because there is one part of me which soars high up among the clouds, and another which clings very much to the earth. To put it simply: there are in my nature materialism, idealism and romanticism. This is what I call a dual nature.

When I go to the theatre or feel stirred up by any other cause, all my reasoning, my criticism, my hair-splitting suddenly become remote, barren and superfluous. Life seems full: and then I drift into another world, full of sweetness and beauty, that does not belong to our sphere. It holds enchantment--the clear beauty of the summer's day with its flowers in bloom and its azure sky.

In this respect, there is a difference between Mummie

and myself. She belongs much more than I do to that a-
zure realm. Yes, I should hate to lose it. But when I
live on this earthly planet, everything is reversed: here
are the books, the cautious, reserved thoughts, the doubts.
There is not a shadow of that other Nelly, pure, sensitive,
lofty-minded. Down here she thinks and thinks, planning
a reasonable, serious life, but the light that shines from
that other world irradiates her thoughts and fancies.

I should like to remain many-sided and to go on belonging to both my worlds, so that the one may not thrust
out the other. It would be dreadful if the whole of me were
to be cast into one mould, but I hope this will never happen. There are all kinds of things in me, and it is very
difficult to know the whole of Nelly.

January 22

Here I sit writing...and suddenly I think; what is all
this? My interest, my life, my aims in comparison with
our earth, as a planet; with all this world, which is called
the solar system; and even more so in comparison with
that immense, abstract, unknown world which surrounds us.
What am I before these all-embracing, vast, incalculable
spaces of nature? What in comparison to them are my life,
my ambitions, to which I devote myself so fervently and
attach so much importance? What are they? A grain of
sand, a speck of dust, despicable, helpless.

January 23

Today I no longer feel this. The futility of our human
interests and the boundlessness of the eternity of some huge
world seem gone.

I tried to think about this, to recall this sensation, but without success.

In my opinion, it is lucky for people that my thoughts of yesterday but seldom come to them, and in any case they are not likely to have them always. These thoughts prevent us from devoting ourselves fully to the tasks which life imposes upon us.

What is my diary? It is a record of my thoughts and feelings. It is curious to note that generally speaking they are young people who write diaries, because their inability to concentrate on themselves, the strength of their sensations, their confidence in the beliefs, which they have not yet lost, make them seek an outlet for their emotions. The old, although they may receive vivid impressions, probably regard them in a colder way than we young people, who are only entering upon life. Youth does not know how to concentrate, and, on the other hand, does not want to confide in others. Hence the diary. The old work out everything in themselves.

January 25

The situation is really terrible! The decisive days for Russia are at hand, "to be or not to be." My vision is too restricted to be able to picture the whole situation clearly. My home life shelters me and I see reality as something, very, very distant. I am mentally short-sighted because, after all, I am but a child: this is the first and most important reason, if not the only one. All the same, at odd moments, I clearly realize the full horror of the position in which our country is placed.

Nevertheless, there have been such cases in history,

and countries have passed safely through similar crises.
What I ask myself is this: shall *we* weather the storm, will
our lives be spared?

February 18

A passionate joy comes over me when I look into the
distance; there, beyond the houses, the towns, the people,
all is radiant, all is full of sunshine.   Then it dawns upon
me that my life will be different from that of the others...
bright, interesting.

I feel so happy then.   If only it could come more quick-
ly--it is still so far away.

But I am able also to look at things differently and then
my gaze shifts downwards, sees more clearly, rests upon
a strange picture.

Then I see young girls, such as I shall become in three
or four years' time.   They live, like every one else from
day to day, waiting for something.   They live drab, dull
lives.   Probably they too had visions of a bright, happy
future, and gazed into the golden distance.   But now....
Where is that golden distance?   Did they not reach it?   *Can*
one ever reach it?   Does it exist really, or only in our
dreams?

For, surely, I am not the only dreamer.   Are they not
dreamers too?   Shall I live on as they do, following the
pattern woven by routine on the canvas of life?   Waiting for
some one?

All children and adolescents probably think thus about
their future life, it beckons to them, it holds out alluring
arms.   But, as time passes, the dreams fade away, one
is content with the present; and not merely content, but

quite happy, once the dreams have vanished.

February 23

How much I wanted to write yesterday! How I longed for my diary! But I could not write. Today there is no one at home and therefore I can put my time to good use. When I am excited or sad nothing soothes me like my diary. If I am very happy my joy calms down, subsides whilst I write. My diary has become indispensable to me.

March 3

Sometimes my inner peace again gives place to the customary tension and then I want to cry. To cry because I feel that I am lonely: that I want Mummie...but in reality because my light-heartedness is leaving me. Yes, life ages, breaks one. Take Raya for instance, she is light-hearted, she lives normally but I am cut adrift. The times have too great a hold upon me, my own life is broken on the wheel.

At such moments I yearn to live as I used to do at home. I want to live as I lived formerly: I want to be free and careless; not to feel this everlasting strain. I am only fourteen! I have the right to be still a child for a little while, to be careless, happy, untroubled.

How strange it is that in the huge machine of life, past present and future, there should be a fourteen-year-old girl who is sitting and writing all kinds of stupid things about her small soul, which to her seems something immense, and that she occupies herself so seriously with something which is really small and of no consequence. But to her it seems all-important and she wholly surrenders herself

to it. How strange is this abstraction; how strange the
isolation of my little life in comparison with that other
which is so immeasurably big.

March 5

I have decided to fight against this feeling of apathy,
which takes possession of me at such moments of depres-
sion. I do not want to allow them. But in order to attain
this result, I must not permit my private life to be affected
by general conditions.

How shall I do this? I shall drive away my thoughts
as soon as they touch upon dangerous ground. I...I shall
deceive myself. Yes, one must confess that in the end it
will only be self-deception. But what matter. It will hurt
no one, and for me it will be better, it will do me good.

One must tell oneself that things are not so bad as they
seem. This is what I want to do and I hope that I shall
be able to accomplish it. I shall not surrender to this
inner voice which faintheartedly whispers to me that our
life is inextricably tied up with this epoch, and moreover
united in such a way that it can never be adjusted; that
therefore everything is at an end and that nothing will come
out of it. No, I do not want this. I shall obstinately tell
myself that--how can I say it most tenderly?--that with
Mummie's arrival all will be well. I shall not allow myself to be influenced by the newspapers, which bring sad
news. I shall not brood over the fact the news is worse
again, and that in consequence our position is all the more
deplorable. In four or five years, all *must* settle down--
and I will leave it at that.

March 11

The world has existed so far; it will outlive this catastrophe, after having outlived so many others. Time will pass...just the same. Everything will pass, peace will reign again, till there comes a new eruption. And for this reason,--and the words are not mine, but it is impossible to find anything that fits the case better--the question does not lie with what will happen in the future, but how we OURSELVES are to outlive this nightmare, hampered with such narrow vision as is ours. If only we could hold out! But the world will survive. We do not know what the future contains, but we can say with certainty that there will be "something." But maybe we shall never know, for we may die before this sanguinary epic has run its course.

October 1

In my dreams, however strange it may sound, I dream at the same time of children and of an independent life, which should be both comfortable and beautiful. The question of woman's fate interests me tremendously. This interest lives in me somehow fundamentally: it is called forth neither by writing nor conversation, but has taken root in me of its own accord.

Is it necessary to add that I believe with all my heart and mind that women have absolutely equal rights with men, because I consider them in no wise their intellectual inferior?

This year I have added to the books on social subjects, some that are concerned with the feminist question, and I shall read them with great enjoyment.

Of course, comparatively speaking, women have not as-

serted themselves up to now as capable individuals. There
are many empty coquettes as well as spiritual nonentities
among them, but, all the same, it is of note that now in
all professions women appear who work on a level with men.

Are there also no empty-headed men? Oh, many! Do
not men themselves encourage the defects of women by con-
sidering them only as amusing playthings? I speak, of
course, in general. There are exceptions but, taken on the
average, they are in the minority.

Does the education of woman prepare her for the serious
tasks of life? The evil of this education is rooted far back
in the centuries. Give women scope and opportunity, and
they will be no worse than men.

I notice that these thoughts remind me of a book I once
read, but all the same it seems to me that they come
straight out of my soul.

Well! The one does no harm to the other.

Yes, woman must have all the rights, and in time she
can earn them fully. At present we have still many women
who are satisfied with their empty lives, but if we raise the
standard, and improve the social conditions of life, which
are connected with her, woman will also rise. Even now
there are many among them who would be capable of leading
a conscious existence successfully. Give them that possibility. When people criticize a woman in my presence, I
never feel at ease, and I realize that they are wrong, but
I have not the courage to dispute with them; I lack arguments and only mentally say to myself, "Wait!"

October 14

Oh, Good God! Is it possible that we shall ever again

enjoy peace and quietness? That life will continue in the old grooves? Now that I am older, how much better I shall be able to profit by it. Then...to travel. The immeasurable ocean, the mountains, the boundless green plains, Paris, London...Nature....People....How all this entices one, calls to one.... But before that, the University in Moscow, the Artistic Theatre, the Museums....How all this attracts me!

And, even if I should fall in love and meet with no response, my life will not suffer from this, I shall arrange it, so as not to depend on love, let alone wait for it as so many girls do. I shall live. If love comes I shall take it; and if not, I shall regret it, wildly regret it, but I *shall* live all the same.

I see in my imagination a small flat furnished with exquisite comfort. Beauty everywhere, softness, cosiness. And I am the mistress of it--a woman and a personality at the same time. I live an interesting life: writers, artists, painters forgather at my house, a really interesting circle, a close, friendly community. I know no picture more attractive than this. I am free, independent. In these surroundings, in which there is even no place for it, I shall not regret love. Life is full without it. It is only the dawn of love which I should miss...those moments, the memory of which beautifies all the life of man.

I see children in my imagination and think with joy about them. The husband is a figure that has never appeared in my fancies, quite a stranger in fact; I have never once thought about him.

On one side I see my little home--on the other I think with· delight of my children.

October 20

I love to stand at the edge of an abyss, at the very
edge, so that a single movement, and...today, stepping
close to the brink of a precipice, although not so deep as
I should have wished, the thought came into my mind that
some day I should die thus, crashing headlong into the
chasm.

My walk today has evoked this premonition. But I feel
it more now, after the walk, than during it.

October 25

Marriage is slavery, it prevents one from surrendering
oneself to that supreme happiness which the initiated call
love--and so I think it is. Human personality must develop
quite freely. Marriage impedes this development; even
more than that, it often drives one to "moral crimes," not
only because forbidden fruit is sweet, but because the new
love, which could be perfectly legitimate, becomes a crime.
Would man and woman be less happy if they lived together
without being married, simply as "lovers"?--possibly not
even in the same house, but meeting every day; in short,
leading the life of a regularly married couple. If they love
one another, what can hinder them from settling down together?

November 5

Sometimes I reflect with horror that when I am grown
up I shall be just an ordinary young girl, with a simple,
grey little life, so that in the end there won't be any difference between me and other people: that all my dreams
and feelings are only the ferment of youth. Deep pain comes

over me and something tightens in my heart. "Am I really but one of the crowd?" I ask myself despairingly. "Just that" is the sad answer. No, I do not want that, it must not be.

My small world belongs to me, it is my own, it is deeply individual. I cannot believe that I do not stand above the crowd, for I have always looked upon myself as superior to it. I thought that I stood apart, that there is much that is exclusively my own and foreign to others.

But my dreams, my hopes of a future life? Must they all turn to dust? Am I like everybody else? That is what I often ask myself. "Only one of the great mass?" Oh, Future! Tell me what thou wilt bring me? Shall my dreams be realized, or not? Shall I go under or rise to the surface? Oh Time, Time, would that it passed quicker! On the whole there is not long to wait--a year, two. School will be over, a more conscious life will begin. What will be Time's verdict?

Once I spoke to Nina. "I think your nature is more complex than mine," she said. And this gave me deep pleasure.

When one hears this from others one is more ready to believe that this may be, than when one only thinks oneself that it is so.

This deep faith in myself, in my nature being different from that of others, seems to have grown with me. I do not think about this all the time, it does not guide my actions, and sometimes I am pricked by a doubt whether this is really the case. But when I begin to discuss the future, the conviction that I am right somehow imposes itself involuntarily upon me. My certainty is strengthened and I then believe in myself and in my plans.

I consider myself a Socialist, and hope that when I grow up, I shall really become one. In the meantime...of what does my Socialism consist? In my views on the form of government, on the situation of the working classes, on the question of political equality. Yes, of course, the Socialists are in the right. There is no doubt in my mind as regards this.

There must not be the abyss which exists at present between the rich and the poor. All must possess sufficient material independence to be able to have their share of higher spiritual pleasures. Is the poverty of the workers, the starvation of their children and the revolting dependence of one class upon the other not horrible, when all have received from nature an equal right to existence and the enjoyment of the gifts of life?

December 21

...while realizing how unjust is the life of the rich in comparison with that of the poor, can one go on profiting by the material advantages which such a life secures for us? That one cannot do so is clear even to a child. This is an important question and an important answer.

The one possesses everything, the other nothing: it is an injustice, and that ends it. If this is my opinion, the least I can do is to discontinue my present mode of life, and bring into it certain modifications which may benefit the people. I am not deluding myself: this is no easy resolution, it is even a hard one: a rich life holds much that is beautiful and my room is full of comfort and of artistic things. To break with all this means partly to deprive oneself in the future of much that is agreeable. I think about it and it is a painful thought: I feel what a sacrifice this implies.

It is serious, it is difficult, but I shall know how to deal with it.

December 27

In Saratoff I received letters addressed to "Nelly Ptaschkina": Mummie never opened them: she did not insist on reading them and if she had asked me and I had refused, she would have been grieved, but would have understood this and not lost her temper: each of us has in one's heart a secret recess, where nobody else is admitted. Father does not recognize my rights as an *individual*. He is my father; perhaps for him I am still a child, but in any case he considers his full right to deal with my correspondence and my "private copy-books." I don't know whether it will be the same thing later when I am grown up. If so, the struggle which is ahead will be more serious than it is today.

January 4, 1919

I have already written somewhere of the beauty that is attendant upon wealth and would be abolished by Socialism. Today I have been to the cinema: the picture was presented in a marvellous setting and while admiring the sumptuous drawing-rooms and the beautiful parks, I had to think of poor tenement-houses with their pitiful miserable inmates. Can one hesitate in choosing between them? Not a single moment. It is the same in life.

A few days ago I behaved horribly, disgracefully. I

bought sweets for a hundred roubles!   How many children
could have been fed on that money at Christmas!

January 9

Is sexual attraction natural, or must it be suppressed?
A most interesting question for study.   What is physical
attraction?   I know that the majority, if not all, will say:
"It is natural."   Tolstoy will remain alone in his opinion.
But this is no proof that he is wrong.

I see life without sexual love.   I do not know whether
this can be, but I should incline to think that it is possible.
It is simpler and more comprehensible; however, not knowing where truth is, I dare not affirm this, but want to think
that it *is* the truth.

The feeling exists.   And at present it expresses itself
in uncouth and misshapen forms.   New ones must take their
place.   That is what I think.

May 22

The farther we go the stronger we feel the influence
of our epoch in more senses than one.   It is very positive:
it has made me reflect on many important questions, like
Socialism and others, it has shown me the real object of
life and has widened my horizon; it has made me more
"practical," more "positive," for everyday life, and has
prepared me better for its different emergencies.

Between the former "Miss Nelly" and the present pupil
of the carpenter Ivan Ivanitch there is a great difference,
especially spiritually.

All this is good, and I am grateful to time for the way
it has helped my development.   But it has also done some-

thing else: all that belonged to the azure realm of dreams and vision, the world of poetry--and there was a great deal of it--has hidden itself in the depths of my soul.

July 9

I should like to weave stories, many stories, about what I see around me: and to tell them in such a way that people who read them would see everything vividly before their eyes; tell them in such a way that the consonance of dead words should come to life from under my pen.

Oh how I want to create, to possess that precious gift of writing. I must have talent for this. I have a few gifts in this direction... only they are but matter without the spirit. Talent, talent, *that* is what I want!

August 30

About six I took some books and went into the Botanical Gardens opposite. It was pleasant to sit there. No one near. The sun, which was already sinking in the west, gave out a gentle warmth through the green foliage, caressingly and timidly as in autumn. Here and there red-brown leaves made splotches of colour. The breath of golden autumn lay over everything, and the life of nature continued undisturbed at the time when history was bringing something new to man.

The thunder of guns and the reverberation of their echo came to my ears in a shrill dissonance; and it was something great that to the boom of the guns of one revolution, I should be reading the history of another that was past. I had Theirs in my hands. The book was living....

Suddenly a roar...a whizzing. I fall down...probably

from the concussion, and remembering from instinct that
one must lie prone to save oneself from the shells I try to
make myself as small as I can, to gather myself into a
ball, and with a faint "Mummie" wait for its bursting over
my head and then...all will be over.   I was on a hillock.
Holding my book with one hand, and still waiting for death,
I rolled downwards.

When I reached the footpath below, I realized that death
--whether it had been impending or not--had spared me.

Mathilde lived in German-speaking Switzerland at the time of the Protestant Reformation. The man who actually brought about the changeover from the reign of strict Catholicism, John Calvin, was Mathilde's cousin. In this selection from her diary, written during her seventeenth year, she speaks fondly of him while revealing his rigidity and moral priggishness.

Mathilde's interest in the events of her day, particularly her feminist awareness of the limitations placed on women by marriage, remind us that the concerns of a girl four centuries ago were not very different from those of girls today.

Mathilde Von Buddenbroch

Geneva, during the Fall of 1536

A new diary, - a new book, - a new biography! What biography? I don't know but it doesn't matter. All people have once been young, have grown old, and have lived out their respective lives. At sixteen, one doesn't ask what the future has in store. One finds joy and peace in living in the moment. Ah yes! How sweet the present is, with its dreams and yearnings, sometimes crossed by such impulsive outbursts of happiness. There are rumblings in the house, goings-on in the family; how this lifts my spirits and inspires me to act. Of course sometimes my parents sigh wearily and become too severe. But they are no longer young, and perhaps when I'm their age I'll sigh in the same, tired way. At the moment, however, all I want is to lead a varied existence, as full of change and excitement as possible. My dear Mathilde, how could you sur-

vive without such constant activity around you? My school
years are over, my younger brothers have inherited my
picture books, and life unfolds its sweet, gay self before
me. It may seem strange that I want to keep a diary, but,
although I am not a celebrity, I claim the right to my mem-
oires. How glad I shall be, at the end of my life, to read
back over these notebooks and discover the meaning of my
modest existence.

To live! The word alone makes my heart swell with
happiness. Life is happiness, and anyone who doesn't think
so has obviously missed the meaning of life. Let me try
to support my argument. To begin with, my father: A respected teacher, a knowledgeable doctor, a man of integri-
ty, a perfect husband and a devoted father. And then, my
mother: a sensible and honest woman, a cherished wife,
the most affectionate of mothers, and so happy to be with
her family. Then there is my sister Lisette: how radi-
antly happy she is! She never argues with her fiance Martin nor with anyone she cares about. The only shadow cast
over this bright picture is that she is going to leave us
soon, at the tender age of twenty. She might have waited
a little while longer to marry, to show her love for us,
but Martin is in a hurry and so of course she is too. Actually, the truth is (though I'll never admit this to anyone
but my diary) that Lisette has been lost to us ever since
her engagement to Martin. As for me, I shall never love
anyone in such an exclusive manner. I love the whole
world, and am enriched by this universal love. But now
I'm getting off the subject, which is that life is happiness
and happiness is life. I have nothing more to say about

Lisette and Martin, so let us speak of Andre, my adorable little brother. Where on earth could one find eyes as smiling as his, or a heart so purely glad? His face is a picture of laughter, although I admit he lacks some common sense for the advanced age of twelve. And now? Ah yes, now the baby Richard, the Benjamin of the family, who we call Richard the Second, as my poor parents lost their first Richard.

Now wouldn't you say I've provided enough evidence for my theory? Especially when you consider that my aunt, who's a widow and supposed to be in mourning, is, on the contrary, as bright and peaceful as a summer day. We call her Etienne Pott, although she was baptised Francoise. I think her example is really exquisite proof of my theory, although cousin John totally disagrees with me. He says that real happiness is locked up inside of you, and is of a severe, unshakeable nature. This hardly satisfies me. I want to expand my limits. As in summertime when everything greens and flourishes, I want happiness to open and ravish me. I know of the pale winter sun which always follows the dazzling beauty of springtime, but this doesn't contradict my theory. If winter is lovely in its harsh grandeur, then surely summer is equally lovely. I am of an extreme nature; I like contrasts and animated living. I'm sure at sixty I will not be the same as I am at sixteen, but I dread deadened sensations. They seem to me like a death warning, and unhappiness is surely the same as death.

Cousin John and I discuss this matter often, although he still considers me a little girl whose ideas are not yet clearly formed. What does it matter? We all make so many mistakes, and I believe a child's viewpoint is as valid as an old man's. I will tell this to John the next time he visits, although I'm not sure how as he intimidates me so, this twenty-seven-year-old man with arrogant airs. The other day he was speaking with my father about the religious reforms which were introduced here last summer. As my father did not share his opinion, John grew angry, until my father stopped him short and said, "Dear John, whoever raises arguments must also learn to accept them." Such conversations are frequent here and I follow them with vivid interest. Mother is too busy with the house work to pay any attention, and Lisette and Martin are too wrapped up in their own world, so there is only me, just graduated from school, who cares about these talks. I don't understand all that is said, but I'm learning a great deal, and I'm pleased to be admitted to these "adult conversations."

The Reformation, by the Good Graces of God, took place. The heavy yoke of Catholocism is lifting and all that remains is to carry out this hard-won battle. That is John Calvin's goal. His work will certainly be great as he is a prudent, decisive and enterprising young man. Of course he is not as handsome as my father, nor as well-built as Martin, but his expressions are really extraordinary! His eyes are fiery and penetrating; his thick, pale face so soulfully serious! His long beard adds austerity to his expression. His aquiline nose, his high forehead, and every detail of his person shows his energetic and domineering character, so far removed from gentleness. Father is certainly kinder and more compassionate than

John. He does not judge so harshly and he respects other's opinions. My father is the best of men and there lies my happiness and my glory.

On principle, I suppose, I will rise early every morning so as to take full advantage of the day. On principle I will continue to keep a diary, so that it will turn into volumes of writing, and, were it possible to always act on one's wishes, I'd make this a general, lifelong rule. Cousin John, yesterday I was asking you if principles didn't make one too dogmatic. You answered, "The lack of principles leads to superficiality and indecision." I accepted this response with great respect. I wonder, however, if one's principles cannot change over time. Can't I embrace today what I rejected yesterday, without being accused of indecision? I will discuss my doubts with Father, who will surely clear them up.

1537

Today I told Mother that I thought John would become a genius. She smiled softly and said, "One does not become a genius, one is a genius." That started me thinking. If we cannot become other than what we are, then what can we hope to accomplish in life? If a man develops from a child, and corn grows from the stalk, then don't we all possess hidden, natural genius? And if God has already chosen his favored creatures, and endowed them with genius, then why do they have to struggle so to develop and perfect their creations? The desire to learn is a human force and I believe that anyone who really puts their mind to it can produce a great work. For example, I imagine that mediocre talents develop in the following way: I write poorly, so, I sit down at my desk and I write, hour after hour, month after month, year after year, indefatigably. After years of such applied discipline, not only will I write well, but I will have mastered the art. To arrive at such a point, one has only to concentrate all one's energy, effort and inner force. Such a study not only leads to a grasp of the science but also strengthens one's character.

So, my dear Mathilde, if you know this all so well, why aren't you a genius or at least in the process of becoming one? In all honesty, I must admit that I am too happy to follow this path. I don't feel the need to concentrate wholeheartedly on the development of my "self." Like the butterfly, I flutter from one flower to the next, tasting life's sweet honey. Had I been born unhappy, perhaps then I'd be more like the caterpillar, inching along, anxious to grow wings. Maybe then I'd become a genius. Oh, Mathilde, you are getting ridiculous. Shut this diary!

So I shut my diary and haven't opened it up again for a long time. The marriage of Lisette took place, amidst a whirlwind of activity. Now there is a heavy silence in the house. I must help Mother with the housework, Andre with his schoolwork, and I must take care of dear little Richard. That doesn't leave much time for writing. But it doesn't matter because my diary will always include what is essential. When I write, my thoughts become much clearer. I would like to write about my sister's marriage today, but the separation is still too painful. I prefer to write about my joys ... such as Schippen Pott's adopted daughter, Annette, who has already become my friend. She's two years older than I am, and much more mature. She's kind and generous and not at all vain. She does not share my high ideals, but seems content with a simpler happiness. Some people are like this; everyone finds their own, special kind of satisfaction. As each songbird chants a different note to create a perfect harmony, so do we rejoice in our separate ways.

Here I am, seventeen years old, being proposed to! My good neighbor Michon, what could you be thinking of? Why in Heaven's Name do you wish to marry me? I assure you, it doesn't appeal to me. My sister's example has hardly served as a guide. I don't want to leave my father, my mother, my brothers and my friends to enter into the confined household of Michon. My father asked me, "Don't you want to consider it awhile?" "Consider what?" I retorted, horrified that my father could conceive of letting me go. He realized my distress and burst out laughing, "All right, my child, I guess you are decided." So, the matter is settled. Although I am dead set against this marriage, I want to understand the meaning of marriage. Dear diary, please help me to discover the truth. Marriage, I believe, is an indissoluble bond which obliges the woman to leave everything behind and follow her husband. Really, it's awful. Could I do such a thing for the love of Michon? Certainly not! To live only with him-- I shudder at the thought. Marriage is a cage which locks you in, and even if this cage is made of diamonds and gold, it is still a cage. Lisette and Martin speak of eternal love and absolute devotion, but I don't want any of it. I want to stay with my parents. Of course I would continue to visit them, if I were married, but then everyone would be reminding me of my wifely duties and telling me about what a husband desires and what a husband allows. My mother is an exception to this rule, but only because my father is also an exception. There is not another man like my father, and that is why I choose not to marry. In any case, I could never be happier than I am right now. I have work, diversions, inspired discussions... what more could I want? My only worry is over poor Michon. He is suffering so from my refusal. I will pray to God to console him and hope this will not be too difficult.

Dear diary, please listen to me because I must talk to you. Tonight I saw Michon at Etienne Pott's house, looking so terribly down-hearted. To see him in such a state made me think, "why doesn't he propose to Annette?" She might be able to make him happy. When I realized that my presence was so painful to him, I got up to leave. What terror ran through me when he started to accompany me. He asked if I had not changed my mind, and, when I pleaded with him not to be so sad, he said, "How could I be otherwise? I'm like a sailor who has caught a glimpse of enchanted shores, but cannot sail close enough to land."

"But what if these shores are actually deserted?"

"Then I wouldn't be so drawn," he answered.

Obviously he was unable or unwilling to grasp my meaning, so I tried to explain. "Sailors are easily fooled by mirages. Often they think they spot paradise, and, upon arriving at their destination, they discover they are staring into the blue sky reflected on the water."

"In other words," said Michon angrily, "You cannot understand my love for you." I remained silent as, indeed, it is true, I don't understand these things. When we reached my house, he turned to me, with great sorrow in his eyes, and said, "So, it's all over for me now, is that right?"

"Of course not," I insisted, "Not all one's desires can be realized. If one chord of destiny is broken, another will surely be woven. The Grace of God is greater than our passing disappointments."

I would have continued, but we had to part. To cause such misery in one man's heart was the second great tragedy in my life. The first was being separated from my sister.

Benoite and Flora are French sisters who both kept diaries during their teenage years. With the threat of Hitler spreading through France, Benoite, eighteen, and Flora, fourteen, begin their accounts of the second World War years.

Born to wealthy parents, Flora and Benoite were used to luxury. When the war crippled France, they were confronted with many challenges and many opportunities for experiences outside the normal sphere of educated upper-class girls.

Their teenage struggles are typical, though their articulation of them belies their young age. Benoite agonizes endlessly about what she is to do with her life and how she is to find a man she can love. Very common themes. Like Marie Bashkirtseff, who also lived in Paris, Benoite could not find a male she could begin to take seriously. Also like Marie, she eventually found herself through work; she is today a well-known journalist in France.

Flora, by all accounts the more beautiful and coquettish of the two, was less scholastically inclined. She, it seems, was able to find love during her teenage years; yet, she was never certain that it was the real thing.

Both girls are incredibly articulate and sophisticated, particularly on sexual subjects. Forced to face death and suffering very early, they show a perception and sensitivity far beyond their years. They are witty, daring, and very open in their love for one another.

Benoite & Flora Groult

May 7, 1940

Flora....I went shopping this afternoon, for a thousand useless little things as in peacetime, and yet we are at war. It's eroding our hearts and minds and I rebel against feeling so unimportant in the storm, a useless spectator and a negligible quantity. I feel as if the only way of participating in these days, when every moment counts, is to keep my diary. To look at my own little war through the tiny telescope of a fourteen-year-old girl who, even in her private life, cannot decide what she wants to do. Benoite thinks we are too silly to have anything to say. I don't care. Let's talk nonsense if we must, but at least let's record our feelings so someday we can live them over again.

May 11, 1940

Benoite.... While I was dining with Pasquale yesterday at Saint-Germain-Des-Prés, Hitler was invading Holland, Bel-

gium, and Luxembourg. The "Great Battle of the West"
was beginning. The Allies immediately crossed the fron-
tier to join the Belgian troops. And meanwhile we were
talking abstract painting and scandal with Pasquale's friends,
some dozen sculptors, writers, and painters, all of them
unrecognized if not failures, which gave them common
ground for bitterness and scurrility. Twelve at table: eighteen bottles of wine. Pasquale undoubtedly attracts me. He
is uneducated; he knows only a few American authors and
the names of cocktails; he mispronounces difficult words and
lacks tact and psychological perception. But his dark des-
perado's eyes make me want to look deeper: Are you there
Wolf? But to seek what? I do not know. It's only too
clear that he has nothing that could hold me seriously, but
why this unexpected attraction to that which shocks me?
It's too rare a phenomenon not to interest me a great deal.

Friday, May 16, 1940
Benoite.... The Germans have entered The Hague, Rotter-
dam is destroyed, a quarter of the Dutch are dead or mis-
sing. The Germans are occupying half Belgium, the Germans have crossed the Meuse, the Germans intend to win
the war in two months. The first week has surpassed
their hopes.

Saturday, June 8, 1940
Benoite.... Paris will fall on the fifteenth. As He predic-
ted. One is beginning to look on Hitler as a God and
it's hopeless to rebel against God. Reynaud was in tears
this evening on the radio.

   He has implored the Americans to intervene. But it's

already too late, if only because of the voyage. One thinks of Paris as of a dear, close relative. What will they do to her?

Saturday, June 22, 1940
Flora.... Oh, I'm ashamed, ashamed of having lost! I should so much have liked my France to win.

Mamma told me today that I was a cowardly spirit. Yes, appallingly so; and, above all, I have no will power. A lack of will power is a difficult thing to remedy. For to have the will to have will power is to have will power already. And when one hasn't any!

Sunday, June 23, 1940
Benoite.... The armistice was **signed** last night. The whole thing is in the bag; France has been sold, but it is we who shall have to pay.

July 1, 1940
Benoite.... I envy the boys now in England. If I hadn't been a girl, I should certainly have gone. In the first place, because the last piece of free France is over there; and then for personal reasons. I, too, am an occupied country, occupied by my parents, my habits, my place in society. I know that my past is nothing but I cannot disentangle myself from its nourishing and nauseating honey. Elsewhere, I could choose freely for myself.

I am tired in advance of the problems which will have to be faced this winter: family life, politics, the presence of the Germans, my examinations, the choice of a profession, my entry into life.... Alas, my attitude toward my

life is like that of a reluctant traveler looking for an excuse to miss his train! In the end, I shall be pushed
forcibly into it, and I'm far too timid even to consider
jumping off while it's in motion.

Thursday, August 6, 1940
Benoite.... There was a ring at the door this morning. I
was in curlers, of course. It was Pasquale, darker and
more untidy than ever, without his uniform which placed
him in our class. He was looking for a room, he was
looking for work, and he wanted to see me. My parents
would have been quite happy at the thought of his being a
prisoner for some time. Alas, it's always the best who
go! I am over nineteen and they keep on telling me so
meaningfully, it is rather late to go on wasting my time.
"Don't forget, the law of supply and demand will tell a-
gainst you after the war," Father keeps saying. Every
boy who passes within my reach--which is a short one--
finds himself automatically under fire from my family. I
am the eligible princess who watches the king and queen
dismiss all the pretenders to her hand on the pretext that
they have not satisfied a series of tests as absurd as they
are insurmountable. My suitors have never yet had the
least chance, and I've always known it in advance. From
the first pressure of their hands, I knew they would not
get far, and any dawning tenderness was tinged already
with the nostalgia of good-bye. How could my mother's
daughter hope to love a boy called Billembois who bites
his nails? ("Can you imagine those shapeless, damp fingers on your body?") For Mamma, everyone has his Billembois side: Egyptians always have a what-d'you-call-it in

their hand, Jews are Jews, dark ones look like foreigners, my friends from the Sorbonne look as if they had come from juvenile court, Pasquale is a failure, Jean-Loup a boy scout, Lenoir a pervert who will leave me pregnant, etc., etc. They tell me I am worth much more than that, but I know they are suspicious of my taste.

August 11, 1940
Benoite.... Joy, joy, tears of joy! I have passed in Latin with a mention.

August 12, 1940
Benoite.... In the euphoria of my university success, I allowed myself to be dragged off to spend a delightful evening with Pasquale. He has found a room in a small, shabby hotel in the rue Bonaparte and I have made promises, which in the light of tomorrow's day seem rather onerous. I am to give him lessons in orthography three times a week and correct the stories he has been writing.

August 13, 1940
Benoite.... Well, no, that sort of thing is definitely not among the terms of the contract. I have discovered that every road leads to the bed, and in particular, a lesson in orthography in a hotel room. Pasquale's burning, abject glance -- his specialty -- gives me a bad conscience. How silly I must look with my lessons! Who am I to refuse him my hand, my neck, my mouth, and the rest next time? After all, it's about time I fell in love. Perhaps I should constrain myself to the ritual gestures so love may come to me at last? Pasquale is certainly no sim-

pleton in this domain, in which I have everything to learn,
and perhaps it would be an advantage for me to undergo
my apprenticeship with a cool head?   Besides,   always
drawing away, stiffening one's body and saying No become
tiresome in the long run.   I have no impression of developing, but merely of withering.   As a result, I allowed
him, between two participles, to kiss me and paw me a
little, my unwillingness being proportionate to the precision
of his gestures.   Pasquale sweated and groaned, and asked
my consent to do things he should do without my realizing
it.   My white silk blouse lost its **virginity.**   My skirt,
when raised a little, revealed disgusting garters.   We
presented a ridiculous and depressing spectacle: the oran-
gutan and the frigid bourgeoise.   My desire to desire died
among such vestimentary awkwardness.   I became, despairingly, myself.   I didn't want to, I didn't want to.   A
dozen times I pulled my skirt down over his hand, which
went on seeking instinctively like an ant returning to the
assault, and in the end I tore myself roughly from his
clammy grasp.   I readjusted my clothes without a word.
"To readjust oneself" after making love must be unpleasant.
After nothing, it is as humiliating and ugly as a snub.
Pasquale sponged his face and shoulders as if he had been
on the point of apoplexy.   Grotesque!   For God's sake,
let's retain some self-control!

"You'll come back, Benoite," he whispered, "I promise that it will not be like this next time."

For the moment, the thought of a next time made me
feel sick. I went down the stairs with shameful alacrity.
How dry and warm it was outside! The passers-by asked
nothing of me.   Little by little, I ceased being annoyed

and began to feel cleaner. "Well, still a virgin! We'll
see about that next time."

Tuesday, August 18, 1940
Benoite.... An intoxicating evening at the Boeuf sur le
Toit, yesterday; intoxicating because of the whisky, of
course. Viewed through my glass, Pasquale had become
the seducer again, and I the prey who wished only to consent. We talked about love for a long time; together with
skiing it's the only thing he really knows about. He re-
proaches me with being unable to shut my eyes, and this
is true. Actually, my ambition is precisely to make love
with my eyes open! Surely it is possible? Or must one
always conceal something from oneself? I have no wish
to remain engulfed in myself. I already spend the best
part of my time there, and the most unhappy. I desper-
ately long to clasp someone on that fragile bridge which
pleasure must construct between two people. I want to
look the illusion in the face, and it will be time enough
afterward, when the rainbow has dissolved, to withdraw
again into my shell and shut my eyes.

Pasquale says that all this is merely words. So what?
Man does not live by bread alone! It is precisely words
that separate us. And we do not succeed in establishing
equal relations between us. Our relationship is that of a
beggar and a joint of roast beef. Not very exciting for
the beef!

Friday, August 21, 1940
Benoite.... In the evening, when the sky fades, I do so
too and almost long for Pasquale's arms. But at three

o'clock in the afternoon, I feel in no humor to listen to
the stirrings of love, and still less to stretch myself out.
Under the sun, I feel ashamed of these shadowy games.
I dislike drawing the curtains in daylight, as if concealing
a shameful act.

Talking of the time, it was three o'clock, and I was
still sitting at my table with Bourciez' manual of phonetics,
and a less passionate work cannot be conceived. Pasquale
telephoned me, inevitably: "If you don't come over, I shall
drink myself to death. You're the only thing that keeps
me alive; you've no right to drop me, you've got a responsibility."

I would have obeyed such a summons from a friend.
Why should I refuse to see Pasquale on the pretext that
he loves me? In any case, I had only myself to consider:
I was no use to anyone or anything. In short, I put my
hat on. But just as I was opening the door to go out, the
fool telephoned again. Poor Pasquale, you lack grace!

"When I think that I traveled fifteen hundred kilome-
ters without a ticket just to see you again, and then you
play games with me. Damn you to hell!" And he hung
up.

Well! I took my hat off again. I did not mind "Damn
you to hell." But I would not accept the phrase "play
games with me." When I came to think of it, the games
seemed expensive.

Five minutes later, he rang up again. "I ask only
one thing: don't stop seeing me suddenly like this. Just
let me get used to the idea gradually that you're never
going to be mine."

Oh, Mother Mary, rid me of these complications!

But Mary made no answer, and I had to swear to go tomorrow. Tomorrow is a long way off, and so many things are happening at the moment.... But I, too, would like to be able to say to him without remorse: "Damn you to hell!"

August 27, 1940

Flora.... Today, I went further than I have a right to do— to the cinema with Van Buck to see a silly film. In the middle of it, he took my hand. I wonder if I did not expect it, for it is a classic gesture. He kept looking at me all the time and said suddenly: "Flora, I love you." It was a delightful thing to hear, and for me it was almost the first time. I said: "It's not true." And I wonder why I pretended not to believe him when I have known it for a long time past. Perhaps, from atavism, the woman in me wanted to savor her victory. Then we came out of the cinema. In the street my incognito weighed on me, and every man's back seemed to be Papa's. We discreetly hugged the walls and he left me at the corner of the Boulevard Saint-Germain. And yet there is no harm in going to the cinema with a boy when you're fifteen! On leaving me, he said once again: "I love you." And I adored being told I was loved in the second person plural.

He has very fine hands; but I do not much like his chin or his shoes. But one has to take things as they come; and, anyway, I have told him about the shoes. He may have another pair hidden away somewhere.

Oh, how I love life! I want to live fully.

August 29, 1940

Flora.... Benoite is boring with her perpetual, "Shall I make love, Father?" Let her just throw herself into the water without knowing how to swim or else stay on the bank in silence. But this eternal regret at not doing what she doesn't want to do, but which she feels would be a good thing if she did... really, it's terribly boring! Tired of hearing her complaining, I finally gave her my opinion. She avenged herself by enumerating the reasons why I shall never be able to keep a man in my toils: my well-known liking for tidiness, which gets me up in the middle of the night to put something back in its place; my few pounds overweight, my sulky nature. She put me through the hoop and, at a single blow, I became the shattered victim though I had begun the conversation as an attacking conquistador. I can never quite manage to get rid of the feeling of inferiority my older sister gives me! I'm good enough at expressing things in the battle of words, but she always beats me in the end.

Tuesday, September 1, 1940

Benoite.... This morning, Flora was ticked off by Papa, and as usual the argument assumed cosmic proportions (on the plane of the family microcosm). With us, everything becomes a pretext for calling everyone in question.

"Flora, you're wearing too much lipstick," Papa said, scrutinizing her through the lower crescent of his bifocals.

"Really, I've scarcely put any on at all." Mamma said nothing, but made signs from behind Papa's back that she had not. Papa was too honest to suspect this.

"Go and take it off at once. I won't have you going

to school made up like a prostitute."

"That's right, darling, go and take some of it off,"
Mamma said with a wink that belied her words. "You
know very well that your father likes you to look like an
orphan."

Papa took up his position at the front door to inspect
Flora's mouth.

"You doubting Thomas!" cried Mamma. "You're always so suspicious! Do you think it's a pleasure to live
with a man who distrusts even his own daughters?"

I could hear Papa by the door getting annoyed and
shouting that it's because girls wear lipstick that France
had been defeated.

"You're always going for Flora," Mamma went on.
"You never speak to Benoite in that tone."

I had not foreseen that. It was too late to escape.
I sat on the cover of the lavatory seat and waited. Mamma carefully pumiced her heels on the edge of the bathtub
and Papa clenched his teeth.

"At Flora's age, Benoite did not wear lipstick. And
Flora will obey me!"

"That's right, it's a dictatorship," Mamma said,
speaking from the wings.

"Dictatorship or not, my daughters will obey me, or
I shall go away," Papa cried, mounting the high horse so
generously saddled by his wife.

"It's rather a question of which of us leaves..."

This meant nothing, but Papa went on. "All right,
you can both go away if you want to! This is my house."

This was an unfortunate argument, a man's argument.
And in the Poiret family we will not tolerate people play-

ing at being men. This time Papa really got going. He
no longer required banderillas. He ran himself through.

"You want to make your daughters into whores!"

"I want to make my daughters into happy women and
not into prudes, like your sister. I like life. You're always in a state of despair..."

"What do you expect? I *am* in despair. Oh, you'd
be happier if I were not here," Papa said gloomily, re-
treating to his room to read the Stoics.

"Oh, the men I could have had if I'd wanted!" Mamma
said. "And when I think that I've spent my life with that
brute!"

September 4, 1940
Flora....It is difficult to return to everyday life when one
has to some extent escaped from it. I have just left Van
Buck, and it is as if I have emerged from a soap bubble
to find myself back on earth again. I felt free, happy,
and adult; he told me he thought of me all day long and
would like to be with me in the country, walking through
the grass. He had written me a letter and he gave it to
me. I am keeping it for when I am in bed.

But as soon as I got home, the soap bubble burst.
Of course, Benoite had not laid the table, and Mamma
sent me to fetch the bread and I had to re-become what
they think I am, what they want me to be.

Oh, what a bore to belong to myself only in snatches
and to have to abandon so much of myself to others! I
wanted to repeat to myself what Van Buck had said to me,
for fear it would disappear into the shadows; but I had to
keep up my end of the family conversation and get up to

clear away the dishes.   After dinner, I said I was going
to work for my examination and disappeared into my room,
to face myself and my letter.

September 8, 1940
Benoite.... At the moment Flora is playing a drawing-room
comedy entitled, "I'm as afraid of a kiss as of a bee..."
She flutters around the lamp, attracted and horrified,
comes and goes, circles around and around and begins all
over again.   She came in very red last night and I played
the cynic with delight.   Her girlish freshness annoys me.
She has a holier-than-thou look about her, this Lady of
the Camellias with the buxom hips, and pretends to have
ineffable secrets.   I went to her while she was undressing,
and asked her rude questions.   She sang at the top of her
voice so as not to hear me and then banged her door.
But since there's no lock, I went and sat on her bed and
interrogated her for her own good.   She hid her head under
the bedclothes and refused to answer.   "Have you left your
tongue with Van Buck?"   She threw her slipper at me, and
I retired satisfied to my room.

September 10, 1940
Flora.... I am fifteen, and I have kissed a boy on the
lips. Oh, impurity! Oh, horror! Oh, disgust! Please
make me ashamed, God.

Saturday, September 12, 1940
Benoite.... Long conversation with Flora last night.   It
started well, but ended badly.   "You're jealous, you old,
dry-as-dust schoolmarm.   You don't know what it is to

have a heart, and you never have known, Mamma said so."
If harnessing men to your chariot, as we say in the rue
Vaneau, is having a heart, well, I haven't got one. In
fact, I haven't anyone to harness. The stallions who have
come my way have been only louts whom I could not even
show off before my parents. As for my chariot, it's only
a wheelbarrow! I have never succeeded in taming a suitable young man. What does this indicate?

And then I do not know how to play the little game
they assure me is essential to attract and hold men--"for
attracting is not everything," as Mamma says with an ex-
perienced air. Men do not like you to leave your stockings around, men like to be managed, men do not like
brassieres held together with a safety pin, and there is
no lack of ravishing and smartly dressed women; men only
really love you if you evade them; men always prefer a
flirt who does not love them to a girl with untidy hair who
adores them; you must never show a man you care for
him, and you must fight on every front to be better turned
out every day than the others. It is true, I do not deny
it, and the examples are legion, and so I am discouraged
in advance. Must one always fight to be loved? "You
must always be on the alert and put on an act," Mamma
says. "To Flora, it comes natural; she has an instinct
for it. But you must learn." Of course it's true that
philology will not help me to attract anybody, and that
men prefer physical good looks to brains! But--is it
laziness or principle?--I cannot make up my mind to tidy
my hair a hundred times a day, to make sure my nose
doesn't shine, to wash out my stockings every night in
slightly soapy water, to fold my sweaters away in the cup-

board instead of throwing them down, to put perfume behind my ears, or not to sit with my feet turned in, to...
not to... to...   All these things, which seem gossamer
threads to Flora, become cables for me.   You do not
learn to be a flirt.   Evidently it's all over with me--I can
only take trouble over things that interest me.

"It's by practicing scales that one learns to play."
Mamma says.   "You must attract all the boys to be able
to attract the one you love when the day comes."

"For instance," Mamma said, "you've got a hat on
your head, but I'll bet you've got a dirty neck!"

"Well, I shall take my hat off.   I long not to wear
hats any more."

"I hate girls with bare heads," Papa said.   "It's bad
form."

"Andre, do you want me to prove that your daughter
has a dirty neck?"

Protest as I would, and admit anything they liked, Flora was sent for the absorbent cotton and some eau de co-
logne.   Flora did not have to be asked twice; our relations
are rather cool at the moment.   The cotton was soaked,
my straw hat was tipped over my forehead, my hair was
raised, and my neck energetically rubbed.

"There, there, there!" Mamma cried triumphantly,
brandishing the pad of cotton, which was of course no
longer white, under our noses.

"But Mamma, it's my foundation cream."

"Are you using black foundation cream now?"

But whose neck doesn't get black in a big city, and
could anyone pass the test of cotton soaked in alcohol?
They refused to try the experiment on Flora.   "For the

moment, it's you we're concerned with."

"Well, Dédé, do you call that having a black neck or not?"

And Papa, who was too cowardly to take sides and never dares defend me, replied: "Well, darling, everyone is master of his own destiny. We shall judge the tree by its fruits.... And if she doesn't marry, she'll look after us later. It'll be very nice."

"Well, I shan't give up. I want my Zazate to be happy, and I shall go on fighting her until she understands."

Having brandished the cotton as evidence, Mamma regretfully decided to throw it away. She put my straw hat and my hair back in place, kissed me pityingly, like some incurable for whom one refuses to despair, and concluded: "You see, Andre, we were wrong to send her to the Sorbonne. The child is not equipped for life, and it's not there she'll become so."

September 13, 1940

Flora.... Benoite, the wretch, has a grudge against me because I am loved. She's nineteen and has never been in love and is trying to spoil for me what I feel and what he feels for me. With hypocritical affection she persuades me to tell the truth; and then, when I have stripped myself bare, with considerable pain, she laughs and turns everything that seemed to me moving into ridicule. But then, why, for Heaven's sake, do I always tell her everything? I ought to know her caustic wit by now and not allow myself to be caught in the trap. I have made up my mind; I shall never tell her anything again.

September 14, 1940

Flora.... Mamma told Benoite today that I was too high-
strung because she had seen on my blotter that I had written: "I love you, I love you, I love you."

Heavens, can it be true?

All the same, I don't care for the physical aspects of
love. I like hands seeking each other and eyes meeting,
but that is all; and I have told Van Buck that I will never
kiss him again. A kiss is too wet, and I cease to love
when I have given it. What is so nice about him, this
friend of my heart, is that he understands and accepts it.
He told me he loved me above and beyond kisses. Here's
a man worthy of my love at last. When one compares
him to all the Pasquales in the world! I could almost
kiss him for accepting the fact that I will not kiss him.

September 18, 1940

Benoite.... One must get married, even if it is only to be
a "young woman" rather than an "Old maid" at thirty.
There is only one term to designate a man of thirty, whatever his personal life may be. A woman, on the other
hand, is qualified according to the use she has made of a
man and by her relation to him. What can one do about
such a monstrous state of things?

A man has only one aim in life. A woman has three,
all contradictory. The mother necessarily encroaches on
the wife, and both weigh heavily against an eventual pro-
fessional success. A woman nine times out of ten has to
base her life on renouncing part of herself, a part of what
life offers her.

I realize clearly that marriage is neither an answer

nor a solution, yet I stupidly desire it as if it could resolve my contradictions. I have no desire to devote myself to my children, and yet I want to have them. I want
to have a personal life and personal work, and yet I shall
have children who will prevent my attaining these things.
I shall need money to be able to live several lives at the
same time and I have every chance, on the basis of prob-
abilities and my natural bent, of marrying a poor man.
My future seems absurd, and I see no way of making it
harmonious. Fortunately, women quickly change their
minds!

September 23, 1940
Benoite....A rainy day. It smells of autumn; I know no
one and am unemployed.

    We resume our winter habits: long evenings "in the
troika," Mamma, Flora and I on the green sofa, the fur
rug over our legs. Papa shouts from his room from time
to time that we are "mad," and that it is one o'clock in
the morning. We laugh at him. It's the hour when we
plot against men.

    "Guess whom I met recently?" I said with what I
hoped was a casual air.

    "The Egyptian," Flora replied without hesitation.

    Had I instinctively resumed the guilty voice of the
period when I used to see Haroun every day? I felt naked,
my least desire transparent. And Haroun was trampled
on and torn to pieces under my eyes owing to my cowardice. It was well known that Egyptians liked young girls.
He did not love me. He was sexually obsessed, like all
his fellow countrymen; and no doubt syphilitic into the bar-

gain.   Panic seized me in retrospect.   Was I incubating
a chancre?   If I had a pimple, I do not think I would ever
admit it.

October 1, 1940

Benoite....I feel at the moment as if I were going down
into a dungeon. Everything seems so organized that I and
France must rot there for a long time to come! We are
hurled into it and walled up. Everyone in our block has
been running to the stores to buy black satinette, for from
now on lights must be totally blacked out. Even flashlight
lenses must be painted blue, showing merely a thin thread
of light "in the shape of a cat's eye."

Finally, the German authorities announce that Jews
must register with the prefect of their region. Everyone
who belongs or has belonged to the Jewish religion or who
has more than two Jewish grandparents will be classed as
a Jew. Every Jewish shopkeeper must place on his shop,
well in view, the words: "*Jüdisches Geschaft.*"

The big bad German wolf, disguised until now as the
Grandmother of Europe, is beginning to show its claws....

Coming home from Galanis, last night, we missed the
last metro at ten thirty. We had to come back on foot
from the top of Montmartre, Papa in front like a sheep
dog and Flora behind, of course, since she had put on her
new shoes and was limping as if suffering from congenital
hip disease. Mamma was carrying our present and future
capital in her Hermes bag, in the form of jewels and bun-
dles of bank notes--fortunately comfortingly heavy. We
must have set a record for the distance on high heels:
forty minutes.

October 3, 1940

Benoite.... On the luncheon menu: roast chicken. When it had been eaten, I wondered, looking at the dirty plates on which the gravy was congealing: "How can I have wanted to eat a chicken?" It is a symptom which reassures me for later. When my blood begins to congeal and I am getting old, I hope to be able to say with the same incredulity: "How could I have wanted a man?" Let us hope desire doesn't survive the possibility of assuaging it.

October 14, 1940

Flora....I went to the Bois with Van Buck instead of going to the Gilberts'; I lied to Mamma. I'm ashamed. I have silently asked her forgiveness. Yet, at the same time, I regret nothing. So, as I say, I went to the Bois. I like Van Buck's wrist and his head like a late bambino's. I didn't kiss him on the mouth. He wanted to, but he did not try again when I lowered my head. We talked, walked hand in hand, and the trees were beautiful. I am madly happy to be a grown-up young girl. My protracted childhood weighed on me and the fact that I am loved is like a consecration of my new state. I cannot, however, make up my mind whether it is Van Buck I love or his love for me. At times, he gets the benefit of my doubt; at others, on the other hand, I am annoyed with him because I don't adore him.

November 1, 1940

Flora....Maternal gossip: Bijou told Mamma today that her son Beaudouin was attracted by me. I'm delighted. I longed for his admiration when we were small at Maisons-Laffitte and he was in love with Benoite and teased me all the time. They were the two big ones and I the little one, the victim; the one to whom the next turn on the bicycle was promised and who ran hopelessly in pursuit of the other two who were only amusing themselves. Ceaselessly I wanted to become part of their magic circle and ceaselessly I was rejected. I remember days that lasted a hundred years, and a feeling of hopeless, despairing loneliness. Benoite and Beaudouin were in league to discover the secrets of life. They had their sources of information and their dictionaries. (Bijou's answer to their questioning was "Recite the 'Hail Mary,' and you will understand.") They used to meet at the bottom of the garden, in a place we called the jungle, share their information and grope their way toward the truth. Benoite obligingly described how a girl was made, and Beaudouin politely reciprocated. My presence would have been tolerated in this secret society only if I had agreed to take part in the lesson and serve as an illustration. For the boy side, there was Daniel, the gardener's little son who could be made use of. But I did not want to know. I wanted to prolong the blessed period of ignorance as far as possible. I felt that it was fugitive and precious, and I found real peace in being in a state of pre-knowledge. Unfortunately, the more Benoite forgot me during the day, when glorying in her association, the more she exerted herself in the evening to tell me what I did not want to hear in the dark of our room. She had promised Mamma that she would reveal nothing to me, but got around her promise by talking to the cupboard. Persuaded that she was keeping her word by respecting the letter of it, she spared me

no detail. Cover my ears as I would, I ended by gleaning
a certain amount of information, and it was already too
much. I remember that it weighed so heavily on me that
I went one morning to tell Mamma about it in the wild
hope that none of it was true, and that Benoite had invented
the whole thing, which seemed far too naked for my taste.
Once again, Mamma understood me completely and swore
that Benoite had in fact lied. She summoned the wind,
the butterflies, and all the poetic euphemisms to her aid,
and life and the problems of reproduction suddenly reas-
sumed in my eyes the grace and poetry that I refused to
allow them to lose. Strong in my recovered ignorance, I
was able for a long time afterward to deny the evidence
and protect myself from reality. I'm very grateful to
Mamma for having realized that I was not yet ripe for
such revelations and that it was necessary, even at the
price of terrific lies, to reconstruct my certainties. I
knew very well in my heart of hearts that Benoite had
raised the curtain on real life; but real life seemed a
rocky coast on which I had no wish to land, and the adults
who struggled on its shores seemed to me much to be
pitied.

Benoite, more sensitive to the poetry of truth than to
the truth of poetry, couldn't forgive my cowardice but pretended to take no further interest in my instruction. But
not for long, alas! She's quite unable to give up on anything.

November 27, 1940
Benoite....My friend Irene is getting married. I shall
lose my only friend. I feel she's taking the plunge. Fran-

çoise, who is jealous, asked her how she managed it, and
as Irene replied that it happened of its own accord, Fran-
çoise is merely convinced she's concealing some kind of
trickery.

In these circles on the Boulevard Malesherbes, girls
write each other congratulatory letters on the occasion of
their becoming engaged, as if they had succeeded in some
exploit.

"I am with you with all my heart in your great happiness."

The same formula serves them for funerals by changing one word. One needs sympathy when someone departs
this life, but not when one becomes affianced. This fem-
inine connivance is rather putrid. I'm sure men say: "Oh,
it's too bad!"

It's wholly unjust, moreover, for a woman is much
better conditioned by her husband than a man is by his
wife. For her, the trap of marriage is a precipice. And
what lies at the bottom of it? Detergents, ammonia, crac-
kers, floor polish, dust under the beds, the chicken to be
put in the pot, care of one's skin and ugly marks to hide,
breasts to be held in place and the menopause to undergo,
while other girls are growing up in neighboring fields.

Brrrrr! How does one manage to survive all that?

December 31, 1940
Flora.... Enter, enter! Today is wash day at rue Vaneau;
we've heated a single bath, an enormous luxurious bath;
it will be up to our necks.

When our nurses pushed us into water into which we
did not want to plunge--"Now, now children! It's past

bath time!"--did we know what a diamond value hot water would one day have for us? The horrible part of it is undressing. Each jersey, each vest or other woolen underwear one takes off is rather like removing part of one's skin, and when one is really naked, one is flayed by the cold. I jostled in the doorway with Benoite to be the first to get in. We have had so many baths together that we have our habits and know who gets the faucets in the back of her neck and who puts her feet to the left. But our feet have grown since we were children, and we were a bit crowded. Then, having quarreled, hated each other, and shoved each other with our knees, our fury turned to joy between two phases of the aquatic battle and we suddenly looked with a stranger's eyes at the two great geese we were, lapsed back into their childhood unawares. We took advantage of our nearness to criticize each other without indulgence: "I like my nipples better." "Yes, but look at your navel, it's like a dark hole." "Don't you think I've got very pretty arms?" "No, they're like those of the Andromaque at the Odeon; I like rather slender arms." "Wretch, it's because yours are!" "I've got the prettiest feet in the family." "Oh, no, you haven't! Those two big gaunt boats?" Mamma arbitrates and pays compliments. "My girls, you're both very pretty, each in your own way."

We rub each other, soap each other, and get out of the water, our skins warm, two Venus Astartes who dare not look back at the gray water from which they have emerged.

Saturday, January 17, 1941

Benoite.... Flora is exquisite just now. She has the bloom

of extreme youth, a down like a plum no one has yet touched. Yet Van Buck rubs himself against her cheeks like a calf against a fence. I, too, am always placed in the position of begging from her. I have learned to ask her for a kiss. This is a very bad habit, which will lead me into trouble!

In the old days she used to give Mamma and me kiss-tickets, which she made herself, giving us the right to one, five, or ten kisses, which we could use as required! Today, she still offers her cheeks and arms, saying jokingly: "Satin, aren't they?" She's always calmly sure no one will be disappointed. Where does she get such assurance, such certainty of deserving homage? I am always paralyzed by the very idea of my partner's possible disappointment. And yet, I also have my supporters--people sometimes feel Flora poses, is too flighty and commonplace. But the main thing is to be sure of one's beauty so as to convince others.

Flora was flattered by the compliments I gave her this evening. As a result she agreed to warm my bed, her legs extended into the remotest corners. She even agreed to stay in it with me for an hour, on condition that she did not have to touch my Gervais bedsocks.

We invented a sort of comic turn. How good it was to laugh and think each other clever. We know each other so well that anything is funny. Can one ever achieve such intimacy with a man?